Advance Praise for

P9-DEN-976

The gospel according to Oprah

"Oprah didn't authorize this lively and information-packed book, but she may one day wish she had. Her fans will love it, and her detractors may even lighten up enough to appreciate Oprah and her influence after reading it."

—*Publishers Weekly* (starred review)

"You won't have to be a fan of Oprah to become a fan of this work. One of the country's most experienced religion journalists, Marcia Nelson, delivers the goods *here* once again. This clear-eyed analysis of Oprah Winfrey as high priestess of America's Judeo-Christian ethos celebrates Oprah's virtues and her gifts to our society; but it never once lets us confuse the uses of cultural religion with those of communal allegiance and private devotion."

—Phyllis Tickle, author, commentator,
and compiler of *The Divine Hours*

"I'm not sure whether—as a character in *Futurama* suggests—'Oprahism' will become one of the world's great religions in the millennia to come. But as someone who has never watched a single *Oprah Winfrey Show* from start to finish, I am persuaded by Marcia Nelson that Oprah could hold her own with St. Francis of Assisi. Now where's *my* car?"

—Mark I. Pinsky, author of *The Gospel
according to* The Simpsons

"Oprah Winfrey has taken a lot of flack over the years for hyping a therapeutic, eclectic, and consumerist spirituality through her media empire. Marcia Z. Nelson helpfully balances that critical account with a respectful rendering of Winfrey's pastoral gifts for listening, encouragement, and exhortation. Gospel or not, the Church of O certainly has an impressive book of virtues: among them, according to Nelson, gratitude, forgiveness, compassion, and generosity."

—Leigh E. Schmidt, Princeton University, author of *Restless Souls:
The Making of American Spirituality*

"Marcia Nelson's clear writing and insightful analysis of Oprah Winfrey's influence on culture and society make this book accessible to a wide spectrum of readers. Nelson highlights the ways that Oprah deepens our awareness of how world leaders as well as the neighbor next door live out the positive themes of the gospel. This book is an uplifting resource for individual readers and also lends itself to use in group discussions."

—Kathleen Long Bostrom, author of *Josie's Gift* and *Finding Calm in the Chaos: Christian Devotions for Busy Women*

The Gospel according to Oprah

Marcia Z. Nelson

WESTMINSTER
JOHN KNOX PRESS
LOUISVILLE • KENTUCKY

Scripture quotations from the New Revised Standard Version of the Bible are copyright © 1989 by the Division of Christian Education of the National Council of the Churches of Christ in the U.S.A. and are used by permission.

The introduction was first published in a slightly different form in *The Christian Century*. Copyright 2002 Christian Century. Reprinted by permission from the Sept. 25–Oct. 8, 2002, issue of *The Christian Century.* Subscriptions: $49/year from PO Box 378, Mt. Morris, IL 61054.

This book has not been prepared, endorsed, or licensed by Oprah Winfrey or any person or entity affiliated with Oprah Winfrey, Harpo Productions, Inc., or related properties.

Book design by Sharon Adams
Cover design by Mark Abrams/Jennifer K. Cox
Cover photograph: © Chris Farina/Corbis

First edition
Published by Westminster John Knox Press
Louisville, Kentucky

This book is printed on acid-free paper that meets the American National Standards Institute Z39.48 standard. ♾

PRINTED IN THE UNITED STATES OF AMERICA

05 06 07 08 09 10 11 12 13 14 — 10 9 8 7 6 5 4 3 2 1

Library of Congress Cataloging-in-Publication Data is on file at the Library of Congress, Washington, D.C.

ISBN 0-664-22942-5

For the Thursday night women's group.
Thanks for listening.

Contents

Introduction

Oprah on a Mission

*T*welve days after terrorists crashed into the World Trade Center and laid bare America's vulnerability in September 2001, New York mayor Rudolph Giuliani organized a service in Yankee Stadium. The service drew together ministers, rabbis, imams, priests, and an audience of upwards of 20,000. This public memorial expression, intended to provide a sense of national unity and social consolation, featured as master of ceremonies Oprah Winfrey. A role that might have been filled twenty-five years ago by Billy Graham, spiritual adviser to six presidents, was played by an entertainer.

Oprah Winfrey, talk show host, film producer, and philanthropist, is not ordained. She is neither preacher nor religious professional. Yet her multimedia empire, built over two decades, has given her the scope and stature of an influential leader. Oprah has a prominent pulpit from which to preach. Her TV show has a worldwide audience in 108 countries ranging from Afghanistan to Zimbabwe. The U.S. audience in 2004 was 10 million, according to Nielsen measurements. Her magazine, begun in 2000, has a readership of 2.7 million and is generally hefty with advertising. (The issues come in different sizes, depending on advertising. The biggest have topped 300 pages.) Oprah's whole enterprise, which includes many media that provide platforms for her gospel as well as sources of income, is vast. Between the movies she produces, books or products she has recommended, her television show, Web site, and magazine, her reach is positively tentacular, touching so many people about so many things in so many different ways over twenty years.[1]

With her conversational ease and casual style, Oprah comes across on the TV screen as personal and personable, both pastor and best friend, authoritative yet approachable. "She is like a personal institution," says Judith Martin, who teaches religious studies and women's studies at the University of Dayton and has written on women and spirituality.

Oprah is, of course, speaking mostly to the nation's women, especially the nation's mothers. Oprah's magazine and TV show advertise products for women. Her TV audience is overwhelmingly female. Most of her book club readers are women, as author Jonathan Franzen understood when he worried that her choice of *The Corrections* might shoo male readers away from his National Book Award–winning novel.

Oprah is primarily the voice of women in the middle: middle-class middle Americans. Many, like Oprah, are middle-aged, or headed there in the next decade. They are people caught in the middle of families, with too many good intentions and an overlong to-do list. These women are trying to manage busy lives and households, address personal and social concerns, and maybe also lose some weight.

Oprah offers lots of things to help. She is an encourager. "Live your best life" is Oprah's motto promoting and summarizing the good life. She offers tools for living your best life: books to read, people to emulate, material things to help (an eclectic assortment of personal or household goods that make up a monthly "O list" of recommendations). The magazine provides "O to go" paper goodies—note cards, postcards, and bookplates—a little bonus feature that adds value to the volume. The journal-like feature "Something to Think About" is a tear-out page for jotting down reflections on questions related to the issue's theme—the month's "mission." "How would you create an 'inner-strength' team?" "How can you be forceful without using violence or harsh words?"

And then there are books. Oprah's Book Club was paradise for publishers, booksellers, and readers. Of the forty-eight books picked by Oprah for her book club in its first incarnation, when it selected contemporary fiction, sales averaged 1.5 million copies each in 1999, the club's biggest year. (The book club now picks classic works of fiction. It made Leo Tolstoy's *Anna Karenina,* originally published in 1877, a best-seller more than a century later.) In this arena, Oprah's roles as saleswoman and guru blended. She prescribed edifying books, many of them by women, and many of those authors women of color. The stories were strong on plot, character, and moral awareness.

Phyllis Tickle, who was editor of religion books for many years at the industry magazine *Publishers Weekly* and likes to describe religion books as "portable pastors," characterizes the Oprah books as "morally sound material, by and large, that is credible and enriching. . . . Like most of what she does, you're the better for having read them. Her tastes are very pastoral as well as literary."

"I have enormous respect for Oprah," Tickle continues. "Anybody who can better the living experience of thousands of people has to be respected. She may not be ordained but she sure is pastoral, and pastoral at a level that has a vast impact."[2]

Although most of the country sees it in the afternoon, the timing of the TV show, at least in the Chicago area—Oprah's home turf—has a morning service feel to it. Go to this house of worship and sit down for an inspiring hour that will engage you and give you a lift. You can even bring coffee to this 9 a.m. ritual each weekday. Even though you are only watching at home, you can feel the thrill of entering something. A disembodied voice-over on TV announces that Oprah's on her way as you see shots of the studio's control room, and then down the studio aisle she is walking, shaking hands, the sound of the studio audience's applause and shrieking accompanying her processional to the stage. An hour-long show five days a week adds up to a lot more pulpit time per week than the average pastor enjoys, and Oprah commands a lot bigger congregation. (Oprah herself used to attend a large Chicago church—Trinity United Church of Christ—but a staff member said she hasn't attended in years.)

On Good Friday in 2002, Oprah's topic was miracles. Her guest was Richard Thomas, the host of PAX-TV's *It's a Miracle,* which every week presents in re-created docudrama form "miracles": incredible and inspirational real-life stories of odds beaten, quirky coincidences, triumph mined from defeat, unaccountable survival.

A videotape unrolls the story of a baby born very prematurely, with no apparent signs of life, who despite all clinical signs and assessment begins to breathe on her own. Two years later, the same girl now toddles onto Oprah's stage holding her mother's hand, offering a flourish of dramatic proof for doubters. The obstetrician is in the audience to say authoritatively that the girl's coming to life is wholly inexplicable from a medical point of view. The miracles show closes with three generations of the gospel-singing Winans family belting out hymns, exactly as in a church service. (The Winans offer their own miraculous testimony—Ronald Winans survived a severe heart condition and is on stage to signal his return to the touring circuit.)

Another 2002 show features Gary Neuman, therapist and author of *Helping Your Kids Cope with Divorce*. A divorced couple sit onstage with their two sons between them. Videotaped segments unfold the story of the parents' divorce from different family members' viewpoints. The mother and father watch a tape of their sons talking to Neuman about how they feel confused and caught in the middle between the parents. Right on the televised spot, this situation is going to be fixed. Mom and Dad pledge out loud that they will get along better and not place their sons in the middle again. "Now that," says Oprah as the segment concludes, "is worth staying on the air for."

She says this periodically. Oprah will be on the air until at least 2011. In 2004, she signed a contract that will extend her syndicated talk show into its twenty-fifth year. Tied as she is to changing cultural topics, fashions, and her own personal changes that have been among the show's subjects, her persistence and longevity represent a successful balancing act of constancy and innovation. Some things change, but her core gospel—improve yourself, make a difference, learn from life's lessons—hasn't.

As Oprah has developed her television show over the years, her use of the medium has established a sense of intimacy within a framework of advertisements. Amazing tales and amazing candor are punctuated by commercials. Confession is the show's signature. Talk is crucial in order to air your mistakes and mend your ways, says Oprah. "The expression of your feelings is like magic," she says.

But expression isn't the ultimate aim of the show. The aim is to make things better. Martin offers a feminist reading of Oprah's mission. "I really think of Oprah as caring," she says. "She has wealth and influence, but she uses it to empower others—and that's a big feminist thing."

When Oprah has a message she wants guests and the audience to grasp, she will ask fewer questions and give more advice. She tells divorced parents who are unable to get along to stop forcing their children to pick sides in parental disagreements. She will sometimes frankly tell troubled guests that they need help. "Tell the whole truth to your wives," she urges seven cheating husbands who have agreed to talk to Oprah about their infidelity while their wives listen offstage.

Oprah often talks about "light bulb" moments or "Aha!" moments (a recurring feature in the magazine also), moments of life-changing revelation. She is explicit about wanting to provide help and resources, about lessons to be learned from her guests: "What I want everybody to get . . . ," she says, referring to what she learned about managing her own health in a conversation with Dr. Christiane Northrup, author of *The Wisdom of Menopause*. When she questions pop star Brandy on a show about the young singer's "spiritual journey," which included an abusive relationship in her teenage years, Oprah observes, "You're gonna save a lot of girls today."

Oprah is a fixer. Indeed, she has a whole team of fixers whose expertise addresses different aspects of women's lives: "life coach" Martha Beck, personal trainer Bob Greene, psychologist Dr. Phil McGraw, decorator Nate Berkus, and financial adviser Suze Orman are among those who have appeared regularly on the show or in her magazine. Whether it's encouraging dieters or redecorating the world's ugliest bedroom, Oprah offers solutions to nagging problems that are blocking someone from living her best life. She is a guide who is there for you, personal as a girl-friend.

"As a moderator of discussions and someone who can generate and respond to ideas, she does great work," says William (Scotty) McLennan, dean of religious life at Stanford University and author of *Finding Your Religion.* "I think of Oprah as a very intelligent woman who is able to draw people out and engage people in a way that is educational and helpful."

Oprah wants to fix communities as well as individuals and their families. She is a consistent philanthropist, with her own as well as other people's money. *Fortune* reported in 2002 that Oprah has donated, mostly anonymously, at least 10 percent of her annual income to charity. In 2004 Oprah was listed by *BusinessWeek* as number 40 on the list of America's most generous philanthropists. It reported she had given or pledged $175 million, estimating her lifetime giving as 13 percent of her net worth of $1.3 billion. She funds the private Oprah Winfrey Foundation. Her public charity, Oprah's Angel Network, promoted on her show and Web site, raised $3.5 million in 1997, its first year of operation. The Angel Network, supported by viewers, has funded scholarships, Habitat for Humanity homes, and grassroots organizations assisting women, children, and families.

From 2000 to 2003, Oprah's Angel Network also sponsored Use Your Life Awards—five- and six-figure awards to those engaged in social change. (Use Your Life funds were also provided by actor Paul Newman, already renowned for his philanthropy through Newman's Own, his food line, and Jeff Bezos, CEO of Amazon.com.) These awards showcased compelling stories and sent out inspirational messages. One recipient was the Red Feather Development Corporation, founded by former clothing manufacturer Robert Young. Young became interested in housing for Native Americans and has built affordable housing on reservations in the northwestern United States. Former prostitute and drug addict Norma Hotaling's organization SAGE (Standing Against Global Exploitation) works with prostitutes in San Francisco, many of whom have been abused and are addicted to drugs.

Oprah wants to fix things her way. She turned down President Bush's request in 2002 to visit Afghanistan to help highlight some of the post-Taliban changes for women and children, refusing to let herself be used for someone else's purpose. She has done shows before on the conditions of Afghan women, but she wants to teach on her own terms.

Some Oprah observers have called her shrewd; others have described her as a control freak. She would probably call it independence. In the April 2002 "What I Know for Sure" column in her magazine, she wrote, "The irony of relationships is that you're not usually ready for one until you can say from the deepest part of yourself, 'I will never again give up my power to another person.'" Personal conviction shades into professional application. The empowered woman is likely to be confident and decisive in business and in personal life.

Self-Disclosure as Testimony

What has etched Oprah's identity most clearly in the public mind is her readiness to draw on her own experience even while exposing others to public scrutiny. Just as she encourages confession from others, she is willing to engage in it herself. She has talked about being abused as a child, and her ongoing battle with weight amounts to a running story line on the show.

"She brings a down-to-earth approach," observes Wade Clark Roof, frequent commentator on American religious trends, author of *Spiritual Marketplace,* and a professor of religion and society at the University of California, Santa Barbara. "I think she talks out of experience and relates to people talking out of experience. Spirituality talk is talk that arises out of experience."

In other words, it is not just talk, but talk that's been tested in life's fires—talk as testimony. As Oprah would say, this is about getting real. This is the language of authenticity. A preference for the freshness and vividness of experience over what can seem like the dull dryness of institutional faith is hardly new, of course. Spiritual renewal has ever been thus. Quaker founder George Fox wrote in 1647 of the inadequacy of the teachings of established religion: "But as I had forsaken all the priests, so I left the separate preachers also, and those called the most experienced; for I saw there was none among them all that could speak to my condition. Oh then, I heard a voice which said, 'There is one, even Christ Jesus, that can speak to thy condition,' and when I heard it my heart

did leap. . . . And this I knew experimentally." Buddha also told his
followers not merely to accept his word, but to test his teachings
by experience. The experience of conversion—felt ecstatically and
instantaneously, transforming sinner into believer—plays a significant role in African American religious history.

Oprah's show is founded on people testifying about their experience. In developing topics, Oprah and her staff routinely seek
people whose experience fits a subject: celebrity fans, women with
untidy houses, makeover candidates. People obligingly write, e-
mail, and call. Oprah's Web site receives thousands of e-mails
weekly.

The show doesn't stop when the TV hour ends. Discussion and
questions continue after the show ends, and this *After the Show*
program is available through the Oxygen cable network, of which
Oprah is an owner. *After the Show* is yet another medium providing resources to pursue an issue.

African American Spiritual Roots

If Oprah's spirituality is a noninstitutional picking-and-choosing
what works from the world's religions, its roots are deep in African
American Christianity. Jamie T. Phelps, OP, theology professor
and director of the Institute for Black Catholic Studies at Xavier
University of Louisiana, identifies significant elements of traditional black spirituality, as well as postmodern eclectic elements,
in the Oprah phenomenon. African American spirituality, says
Phelps, "understands we are all human beings. If you're generally
into black spirituality as holistic you have to love everybody—that
makes white people very comfortable." Phelps suggests another
reason for the comfort level of white viewers and fans with Oprah.
The figure of the nurturing television personality echoes the historically and socially accepted figure of the nurturing black
female. "She is the good black mama who takes care of white
kids," Phelps says.

L. Gregory Jones, dean at Duke Divinity School, agrees that
Oprah's roots in the black church experience lend the television per-

sonality some of her authority. "It enhances her credibility on issues of spirituality, given the prominence of the black church," he says. "There is a cultural presumption of credibility that she can trade on."

Oprah's attempt to transform community by promoting individual transformation is also a way of placing individuals within a larger community. There can be no separation, no isolated search for individual perfection. The individual's betterment leads to community betterment. Individual spiritual life, and renewed life, is expressed in community and community renewal. The traditional black church has always addressed community ills, expressed community cohesion, and been a refuge of liberty that is personal, social, and spiritual.

"There is a personal relationship to God that has to flow over to concern for community," says Phelps. "It's not a personal 'getting holy' but getting into right relationships with the community."

If Oprah can be said to have a theology, it is the theology of story. Like religious teachers who used stories to make their points about how to live, Oprah also uses stories: the novels in her book club, the life stories of her guests, and her own life story. She uses these stories to teach values. They provide an opportunity to learn something, either from a book or from life's book. Like a refrain, she asks guests: What did you learn from this? She also involves her audience, asking rhetorically: What would you do? Would you judge? Would you forgive? This helps to involve the one hearing the story, making it more personal. Story is memorable, it can be shown on TV, and it's easy to understand. Storytelling is an ancient art, and book-loving Oprah knows and takes advantage of its power.

A Little List

Consider these ten reasons why Oprah is a compelling and successful spiritual teacher in spiritually eclectic and ever-practical America:

   1. Oprah is very human. She admits to struggles with human temptations, like food. This distinguishes her from lots of other religious figures in the culture.

2. Oprah acknowledges the reality of suffering and wants to do something to relieve it. At her prompting, people regularly tell wrenching stories of being abused or victimized. Trisha Meili, the woman known for many years as the Central Park jogger and a symbol of urban crime after a savage attack on her in New York in 1989, broke her public silence for an interview with Oprah in 2002. Oprah followed the September 11, 2001, terrorist attacks with an extensive series of shows emphasizing understanding, coping, and healing. Her September 11 six-month anniversary show in 2002 featured World Trade Center survivor Lauren Manning, a victim of serious burns. Suffering happens. Talking about it and exploring survivors' resilience seems to help.

3. Oprah provides community. You can log on to her Web site (http://www.oprah.com) and pick from hundreds of support groups and message boards. You can go to a bookstore, look for a book with an Oprah Book Club logo, and know that lots of others are reading that very same book. You can subscribe to her magazine and know that you are among a community of nearly three million people reading the same advice columns as you.

4. Oprah encourages self-examination. The traditionalists might call it examination of conscience. A daily Examen is a technique for Christian spiritual development. Oprah would call it journaling or "Something to Think About," her magazine's feature that presents questions for reflection.

5. Oprah teaches gratitude. St. Paul says, "Do not worry about anything, but in everything by prayer and supplication with thanksgiving let your requests be made known to God" (Phil. 4:6). Oprah encourages people to write those requests in their gratitude journal, a daily record of things or events for which you feel grateful. "The gratitude journal is a wonderful idea as a supplement to people's already formed spiritual life," says Jones at Duke Divinity School.

6. Oprah is easy to understand. She keeps it simple. She uses little words. You'll never hear "postdenominationalism" or "hermeneutics" or other religious jargon on the show. Her regular magazine column, called "What I Know for Sure," is simply written, and filled with her experiences and reflections on those experiences. Oprah keeps it simple, cutting through words, summarizing, highlighting, recommending, trading on the trust she has built up over the years, using what people who study influence might call "moral capital."

7. *Oprah listens.* Being heard is good for well-being. Catholics put this to work institutionally in what is popularly called confession and formally known as the sacrament of reconciliation. This same principle is at work in twelve-step programs, which require confession of character defects as a foundation for responsible change. Confess, repent, and be healed. As Dr. Phil McGraw might say, "Own it."

8. *Oprah teaches generosity by highlighting and encouraging role models.* Oprah profiles those who make a positive difference. She and her viewers also bankroll some of them, through Oprah's Angel Network. The Angel Network makes it easy for viewers to do something about their charitable impulse—namely, send in a check. The Web site also allows them to find information about volunteering. Oprah herself has given away millions.

9. *Oprah explores forgiveness, and tries to demonstrate that it is possible and how it is possible.* She regards it as a tool for survival. She has regularly spoken with survivors of crime—people who have lost loved ones or have themselves been victimized— and returned years later to check on their progress.

10. *Oprah is a reminder service: a reminder of what is good, what is important, what one person can do.* In this information-glutted culture, the busy need reminders to help them remember what's important. My husband, a pediatric nurse in a suburban Chicago hospital, gets an occasional small dose of Oprah. In patients' rooms during morning hours, *The Oprah Winfrey Show* will sometimes be playing, watched by moms sitting with their sick children. He recently asked one *Oprah* watcher what she liked about the show. She watched, she told him, for the information: safety for children, decorating, and the like. This information was not necessarily new, she explained, but she liked to be reminded.

This book elaborates these ten reasons in the chapters that follow. Before I paid close attention to her work, I would not have called myself a fan, mostly because I don't think of myself as any-body's fan. As a religion writer, I am uncomfortably aware of the relationship between the words *fan* and *fanatic*, so it's a term I shy from. I wrote this book because I wanted to understand what Oprah was doing that so many people admired and responded to. I tried to discover that by watching her show for a season, reading her magazine, and talking to admirers as well as people who don't par-ticularly like her.

I wanted to understand what kind of role a famed talker might have in our American conversation about values. As a religion writer, I have listened over the years as *values* has become a pop-ular political term in our culture wars: family values, moral values. As a person of faith, I tend to identify values with virtues. *Virtues* is a term that reminds me that this conversation about values is more than a contemporary political shouting match. It reminds me that there is a treasury of time-honored teachings about how we should live that religions at their best have provided. Virtues describe qualities of character seen in action: gratitude, generos-ity, compassion.

If the word *values* suffers from some imprecision in usage today, though, it does have one advantage. It's not necessarily tied to religion. A growing number of people today say they are "spir-itual but not religious," because they are turned off by what they see as the "dark side" of organized religion. History contains reli-gion's track record of cruelty as well as compassion. So while *val-ues* is often used today as a code word telegraphing conservative political views, it can also mean something more expansive: what someone considers important whether he or she is religiously observant or not.

Here is where Oprah fits in. She speaks about values: things that are important to her and things she wants to be important to all of us. They are rooted in religion, and she has been shaped by reli-gion. But she is not a religious figure. Oprah has transformed her-self and what she is doing in a series of makeovers over time, and yet there is a core of consistency in what she does. She has made herself into an exemplar of values, a shaper of tastes, and an enter-tainer. All three of those functions work together. People wouldn't listen to her if she weren't entertaining. Her influence would be smaller if she hadn't ambitiously tackled basic issues of cultural values and tastes, offering some guidance. She translates what religions would term transcendent into something that is inspiring but secular. She would call it a vision of possibilities. She has tried to develop her own unique language, which means talking about values in a secular and inclusive sense in a religiously pluralistic country.

At their core, religions too offer a vision of possibilities; they are one established, systematic way to help people become their better angels. Some find this too sentimental or choose to take routes other than religion to discover meaning, but for many people this vision provides a reason to get up in the morning.

Oprah was off-camera but on-pulpit at Cleveland's Olivet Institutional Baptist Church when she told two thousand people gathered there in April 2005 that God helped her see the possibilities in her life. In her earliest teenage years, her future looked especially unpromising. At one point she was headed for a juvenile detention home. "The voices of the world told me I was poor, colored and female," she told the congregation. "But God had another vision for me."[3] Her own belief in God offered Oprah a vision of her own possibilities. She evidently listened.

Chapter One

Oprah Is Very Human

*E*ven if they don't watch *The Oprah Winfrey Show* or consider themselves familiar with her work, many perceive Oprah as a force for good or think of her as authentic or approachable, a down-to-earth person they might like to know. She has a stature and reputation for personal integrity that extends far beyond whatever her own organization could construct. She wields influence and visibly shapes opinion. She is powerful—but she also comes across as human, unlike many other people of influence.

She has a platform to talk about things of the spirit that many religious leaders would die for, especially because she doesn't have to be perfect. She gets to make mistakes. From televangelists to bishops, religious leaders don't have that margin of error. Scandals within organized religion—pedophilia, financial fraud, sexual indiscretion—periodically reinforce skepticism, even cynicism, about organized religion and religious leaders. Though her self-confessed mistakes are far less serious, by contrast, Oprah has room to fall down, pick herself up, and try, try again. Her quest is for improvement, not perfection. In keeping with a religious understanding of human nature as inherently flawed or limited in some way, Oprah is a flawed human who profits, literally, by her imperfections. People can relate to her flaws: We have ten pounds too many, a big bottom or some other physical imperfection, relationship difficulties, bad hair days, or a personality trait we'd like to change. If Oprah hadn't made and experienced mistakes, she wouldn't be who she is. Sociologist Eva Illouz writes, "Oprah's persona seems to have emerged not in spite of but *precisely thanks to* her failures. . . . Oprah Winfrey casts herself as the condensed

1

version of the problems that plague the most ordinary of women: lack of self-esteem, sexual abuse, overweight, failed romantic relations."[1] Longtime business associate Jeff Jacobs once told *Entertainment Weekly*, "People of all backgrounds identify with her because she's never shied away from showing herself, warts and all. They know she's made mistakes and she will make mistakes, just like everybody else."[2]

Oprah taps into nagging dissatisfactions. She offers a way to transform your own unhappiness into happiness. Her own failures and their overcoming have made her successful. The story of her rise from humble beginnings to billionaire status is well known, and she routinely refers to her humble origins. That story resonates with anyone who has even a passing acquaintance with the American dream, including many who live in the hundred-plus countries where *The Oprah Winfrey Show* is televised. Her autobiography and the personal details she shares with viewers are confessional. They are proof of her flawed humanity. She has fashioned an image of integrity through her own confessions of weakness, through the appearance of discipline and its inevitable lapses. She is Eve, yielding to temptation. She told Mike Wallace on the television news show *60 Minutes* in 1986, shortly after *The Oprah Winfrey Show* was syndicated nationally, "The reason I communicate with all these people is because I think I'm every woman and I've had every malady and I've been on every diet and I've had men who have done me wrong, honey. So I related to all of that. And I'm not afraid or ashamed to say it."[3]

Right before Your Eyes

As someone with a keen eye for story, she can spin endless variations on her personal weight loss saga, which has enough details to fill a book by itself.[4] The same essential story changes over time, one's eyes can confirm what she is saying, and it seems realistic. People do change over time. They succeed and they fail. Two steps forward can be followed by one step back, making for watchable drama. Over the course of Oprah's television career, her weight has varied by almost a hundred pounds. Viewers watched her shrink using a liquid diet in 1988, and on November 15, 1988, she wheeled a red wagon onstage containing sixty-seven pounds of animal fat to graphically illustrate her weight loss. It didn't last. Subsequent weight struggles continued to provide material. Dieting allowed Oprah to develop programs and themes that could interest and change. To lose weight, you could "get with the program," the slogan that summarized her work with personal trainer Bob Greene and was a hallmark of the show in the middle 1990s. Another approach was more psychological. You could understand the reasons for your eating, which she described as "emotional eating," the subject of shows that explored the psychological dimensions of why weight loss doesn't last. Her weight diary was another technique; so were relationships developed with personal chefs. Ways to address weight issues yielded lots of shows and also made an indelible public impression of Oprah as a struggling human being.

Oprah's weight is more than extra pounds. Oprah's weight affirms that we're all flesh, sometimes a little too much so. She almost needs to fail—to put weight back on or experience some other failing—in order to retain her humanity. She *can* be too thin or too rich. She is very rich, a condition to which not many can relate. Far more relate to flaws and a wish to triumph over them.

For Oprah, failing has its uses. It can become another story from her life of struggling and overcoming. Oprah has to fail a little but triumph a lot. She continues to show this can happen, and in many instances provides specific instruction how to overcome a problem: Join Oprah's boot camp to lose weight, ask Dr. Phil or one of her consulting experts, start to change by asking yourself questions. Oprah herself stands before your eyes, proof of her message that change is possible. She is about successful change even while failure provides tension, complication, and a dose of reality into the running stories of problems and solutions. Some problems will be resolved and some will recur.

Oprah walked onto the national stage with two personal issues evident from the beginning: her weight and her sexual abuse as a child. Both have provided her with lots of material and a way for many to identify with her. From the days when *The Oprah Winfrey Show* began national syndication in 1986, both subjects have been explored repeatedly and personally. On the November 10, 1986, show, "Sexual Abuse in Families," Oprah says in the show's opening remarks, "I speak from personal experience, because I was raped by a relative. . . . I'm telling you about myself because when it happened to me, I couldn't tell anyone, because I thought it was all my fault." Oprah then interviews two women and their fathers who molested them, along with three experts. The show's format allows comments from the audience and from callers, all of whom on this day spoke about their abuse. Oprah concludes by providing a number to call for help and information. That very early show contains many of the elements that still structure shows twenty years later: confessional or personal remarks from Oprah, ordinary people sharing their experience, longer interviews at the beginning of the show, a conclusion that brings out the point of the show, the offer of resources to help, and Oprah's closing gratitude.

Oprah is never distant. Not only does she give information from her experience, she also famously shows emotion, crying when sad, displaying enthusiasm that seems contagious, often opening shows with an exclamation of how much she loves to come to work as her audience cheers. The feelings that animate her talk get her words noticed. When she famously exclaimed on a 1996 show that information about mad cow disease "stopped me cold from eating another burger," the beef industry heard that remark and, fearing too many others would hear and agree, slapped her with a lawsuit, which she won. Her spontaneity made for problems in her early career in news broadcasting. An ordinary journalist is expected to stay out of stories and not reveal emotion. But biographer George Mair says she couldn't do that when she became a news anchor in Baltimore in 1976. "Oprah couldn't report the murders, rapes, and mayhem without compassion. Her feelings for the victims of disasters and crime came across television clearly, and she was moved by tragic stories."[5]

Oprah has said that she realized she could be more successful by being herself than by trying to be like newswoman Barbara Walters, who in 1976, the year Oprah went to Baltimore, was hired by the ABC network to coanchor news. Yet Walters, who could ask both personal and policy questions of leaders she interviewed, blazed a trail for women in broadcasting that Oprah followed and acknowledged. The very quality that didn't work for Oprah in news reporting became her biggest asset in the world of the talk show. Her ability to listen and respond with quick wit and ready emotion distinguished her and helped forge her identity as authentic and "real." She has developed and refined her public expressive style for more than a quarter century, interviewing every kind of person, presenting a wide range of topics, and appearing invariably attentive, never bored.

Yo, Girlfriend

Oprah's style of talking is also distinctive for its girlfriendly confidence sharing. Her self-disclosing talk is laced with personal details. People know about her longtime boyfriend Stedman Graham and about her best friend, Gayle King. Oprah regularly acknowledges the role of her production staff in providing her with information ("My producers tell me") about whomever she's interviewing. That suggests a sense of collaboration, even modesty on her part. The showcasing of Oprah's favorite things and books she recommends also convey a message about her tastes that contributes to one's sense of being familiar with her. Countless details—from secrets to preferences to personal history—make her seem like someone you know. Her television manner is just plain likable.

Linguist Deborah Tannen, whose book *You Just Don't Understand: Women and Men in Conversation* helped shape popular understanding of how men and women speak, wrote in *Time* magazine that Oprah's style of talking, with disclosure of secrets and back and forth flow of conversation, mirrors how women talk with friends. "Girls' and women's friendships are often built on trading secrets. Winfrey's power is that she tells her own."[6]

Over the season-long course of watching Oprah on television, I felt myself getting attached to her in some of the same ways I might identify with a character in a novel. I noticed when she had a cold, felt disappointed when she did a show about something that I really didn't care about, felt glad when I thought she nailed a topic that was important, laughed, and often felt that she spoke my mind when she said, "I just don't get this," before asking a question of some cheating husband or gambling addict. I cared about some things I wouldn't have seen or known otherwise, from actor Jamie Foxx's inspiring grandmother to the rape of women in Congo. Her tastes aren't like mine, but I always checked out the shoes she was wearing. For anyone attuned to style and visual effects she is a kaleidoscope of change, looking different each day. Close as your TV or computer and yet not someone you buy a gift for, Oprah represents what playwright, actor, and show guest Tyler Perry calls a "familiar stranger"—someone you really don't know, but you feel you can trust her.

Oprah has been termed an American icon. *Time* magazine's "100 Most Influential People" for 2005 lists her in its "heroes and icons" section. Her physical image is unique, marketable, memorable. Icons have been used within religions to teach, to humanize the divine, to make it easier to concentrate. An icon humanizes something transcendent, making it easier to understand and relate to. Oprah has said her picture is always on the cover of *O, The Oprah Magazine* so that she doesn't have to bother seeking cover models. But her face on magazine racks has an iconlike draw. It is familiar. I am every woman, Oprah has said. Look at me and see yourself and your concerns. That's a bold claim that not everyone buys. But millions see, if not their exact image, at least something that reminds them of their own human hopes and flaws.

Chapter Two

Oprah Acknowledges Suffering and Wants to Relieve It

*W*hen bad things happen to good people, those people often ask: Where was God when this (genocide, tsunami, cancer) happened? The question is probably older than Job and his trials, a biblical story that is also a powerful meditation on suffering. The question is older than the Buddha, whose Four Noble Truths explain suffering and promise an end to it. Religions usually offer some response to the mystery of suffering.

One of Oprah's most recurring themes is suffering. One form of suffering she has focused on is abuse in families, especially child sexual abuse. It springs from her own experience of sexual abuse as a child, and has been the subject of numerous episodes of *The Oprah Winfrey Show* since its nationwide beginning in 1986. Her work has repeatedly exposed suffering in its many forms and sought to alleviate it. Because of this, critics have sometimes accused her of profiting from other people's pain. But her goal has been consistent over the body of her work: to make things better. If Oprah shows suffering, she also shows reasons for it and responses to it, just as religions offer. In this way she can also justify to herself and her viewers that showing suffering is not just voyeurism. And in this way, she offers answers and consolation, a system of meaning, just as religions do.

Television is one place people go for answers. Religious and spiritual themes abound there. "Meaning systems are not coming from guys standing up in the pulpit," says Wayne Thompson, a sociologist who studies religion and the media. "TV has to be one of the most important sources." Because the medium of television as she uses it has great power to move and to reach around the world, Oprah can use it to show suffering, teach what suffering means, and, more importantly, show how to respond to suffering. She doesn't need to preach.

In 2002, Oprah traveled to South Africa to produce a "Christmas Kindness" show that aired in 2003 and was followed up in 2004. The 2003 Christmas show focused on AIDS orphans in South Africa and bluntly asked for assistance. "What I wanted for you to see is the extreme need for us, for everybody who hears this today, to do what you can to help," Oprah told viewers. The 2004 show followed up some of the stories presented in 2003, covering South African schools and social programs, and showed where $7 million, collected by Oprah's Angel Network in response to the earlier show, had gone. Singer Alicia Keys and actor Brad Pitt appeared in 2004 to talk about AIDS and access to medication. Pitt was on tape but Keys appeared live to talk with Oprah, who gave the singer a check for $250,000 to support Keep a Child Alive, a program that provides AIDS medicine to African families. Keys said that having an impact on the lives of those she met seemed easy despite the size of the need. "I couldn't believe how simple it was," Keys said, sounding a you-can-do-it-too note.

The efforts of much less well-known individuals were also shown. A California film producer related her story of going to Africa, as did a photographer who went to Africa to shoot school portraits for children. "I see inspiration," the photographer said in describing his experience.

Oprah concluded the show by facing the camera and thanking her viewers for their contributions. "It's our human family that is suffering across the ocean," she said. The last word went to children, with film clips of South African schoolchildren saying, "Thank you."

The South Africa shows exemplify Oprah at work informing and moving viewers about suffering. For her, suffering is not a general philosophical question; it is a particular condition being experienced by individuals, in this case children in South Africa who have been orphaned by AIDS. The remoteness and magnitude of the issue—South Africa has 12 million AIDS orphans—is scaled down and humanized into the faces and stories of individuals. Oprah's shows selected a half-dozen educational and social-aid programs reaching a vast group of children. They showed a variety of solutions to the problem and people who have taken action. Also included was an interview with South African archbishop Desmond Tutu, who provided a moral framework for this action. Hence, Oprah doesn't need to preach because she's got a preacher on hand.

"God wants the story to be beautiful and that we live happily ever after," Tutu said. Tutu's credentials and experience give weight and credibility to his simple statement about God's will, the subject of centuries of profound theological debate. That we should live "happily ever after" is a statement that echoes for anyone who has heard the phrase in childhood. The Tutu interview came right before the hour-long program ended. Oprah closed with gratitude, not with hand-wringing about the vast scope of the problem or blame upon the South African government or pharmaceutical companies that aren't making enough affordable drugs available.

Sociologist Eva Illouz says that Oprah's TV show "has taken on the vocation of relieving a multiplicity of forms of suffering."[1] One of the ways that religion explains suffering is to give it redeeming value. It ennobles character or makes you better: "No pain, no gain" is shorthand for a profound theological teaching that many believe. That suffering has redemptive value is a part of Oprah's message that grows from her Christian religious roots. The suffering of Jesus on the cross is central to the message of Christianity that suffering redeems. And so Oprah's focus on suffering and its purpose echoes that religious teaching.

African American spirituality acknowledges the suffering that is part of the history of blacks in America, provides a refuge and an explanation, and offers some answers. That history and spirituality shape Oprah's understanding of the meaning of suffering. Illouz puts it this way: "Oprah Winfrey has derived her insistence on endurance, self-help, and the perfectibility of the self from African American culture, in particular, from an interpretation of the world that helped make sense of and bear suffering."[2]

The African American spiritual and cultural tradition that has shaped Oprah also sees suffering as a collective experience rather than merely a private and individual one. "Community is significant," says Jamie T. Phelps, director of the Institute for Black Catholic Studies at Xavier University. "It helps you, nurtures you, sustains you, and you in turn are to nurture and sustain the next generation."

That individuals give back in order to lift up others is a strongly felt obligation in African American spirituality. "If you make progress, you have to help your cousins make progress," says Phelps. Transformed individuals transform community, so self-change flows into social change.

"I Alone Have Escaped to Tell You"

The messengers who tell the biblical Job of the calamities that have befallen his family also sound a note of survival. Those who survive suffering have stories to tell, stories of resilience that fascinate for many reasons. Ask any fan of *Survivor*, the granddaddy of the reality television show genre. These stories arouse curiosity and ultimately provide reassurance. They engage vicariously. They are dramatic stories that build tension through conflict that needs resolution. They have a beginning, middle, and end, preferably quickly if they are to suit television. Stories of triumph over odds inspire as well as engage.

Survivors are often idealized as superheroic: strong, courageous, quick-witted, exceptional. Oprah offers a twist on this understanding. Her heroes have everyday faces. They are ordinary people who have made unusual decisions: strangers who donate organs, high school students who stop an attacker wielding a knife against their teacher, a neighbor who saved a two-year-old from a pit bull. She is interested in exploring and showing what makes a "real-life hero."

In her gospel, survivors aren't necessarily superheroes. Like many of her guests and most of her viewers, survivors are ordinary people. But they have experienced something extraordinary. Oprah asks—pushes—them to find a lesson and share it with others. Their talk is testimony, and it provides a community improvement forum. The hard-won knowledge helps others who might find themselves in similar situations. A college-age woman tells Oprah and viewers on the September 30, 2004, show, "This Show Could Save Your Life," that she was able to resist rape thanks to a story she saw broadcast on Oprah the same day as the attempted rape. Individual experience adds to group knowledge.

Oprah is known for her concern about the suffering of children, as her work and her biography make clear. Oprah's abuse at the hands of male family members is a defining fact of her life story, and she wove that early into her subject matter. "Sexual Abuse in Families" was broadcast on November 10, 1986, two months after her show began running nationally. "Truddi Chase—Multiple Personalities," on May 21, 1990, features a woman who developed ninety-two personalities as a result of childhood sexual abuse. "I Shot My Molester," on October 1, 2004, presents both a convicted child molester and his victim, his stepdaughter, who questions him about his reasons for molesting her. The second part of the show presents the story of Janice Clark Smith, sentenced to seven years in jail for killing her own father, who had molested her and her two sisters. This show also promotes the film version of the novel *Woman Thou Art Loosed,* in which Oprah acknowledges her financial investment. Bishop T. D. Jakes, popular author and pastor of the Dallas area megachurch The Potter's House, appears on the show and explains the allusion to Christian Scripture the title contains. The words from Luke's Gospel are intended to convey liberation from the trauma of domestic abuse. Oprah notes that some people in her studio audience are familiar with the Christian reference. "All the Bible reading people back there are going, 'Yes, it is,'" she says.

Oprah has made abuse the subject of dozens of shows, exploring multiple cases and angles. Her shows try to show who abusers are, how they work, what happens to children who are abused, and what to do to get help. She is explicit about these goals. Child sex abusers and their victims have faces; this is what they look like, she repeatedly tells her audiences. Her abuse stories include reporting drawn from public records of cases. This factual information is blended into an emotional tale—sometimes using footage that dramatically recreates an event—intended to teach about the subject: Avoid this behavior, don't make these mistakes, know the signs.

While child abuse has been a career-long concern, Oprah has also explored global instances of suffering, again by giving suffering a face that makes it easy for people to relate to. The December 2, 2004, show, "Children Who Shook the World," uses that technique, presenting a gallery of children's faces that have memorably defined conflict or social problems. Early in this show Oprah states the lesson, which she will reiterate a few times: "I believe each of us holds the deepest hope that each of our lives really matters." The program begins with the story of an Ethiopian girl whose picture, shot in 1984, helped to dramatize the starvation ravaging that African nation. Oprah then introduces Birhan Woldu, calling her the girl who put a face on famine. She survived and is now twenty-three. Also on the show is Canadian Broadcast Corporation correspondent Brian Stewart, who first spotted Birhan. Addressing him, Oprah says, "As a journalist you want your words to be heard and to have people see things differently." Those words echo the way Oprah describes her own aim: to get people to think about things differently.

This show highlights other instances when children's faces have come to stand for issues or events: Kim Phuc, the nine-year-old Vietnamese child photographed running from a napalm attack in 1972, a picture that helped sway American sentiment against involvement in Vietnam; Ryan White, a teenage AIDS sufferer whose struggles to receive an education in Indiana provided Americans with an education about AIDS; Megan Kanka, whose 1994 murder produced a law requiring a public registry of convicted sex offenders; Chinese baby girl Mei Ming, featured in *The Dying Rooms*, a 1995 documentary about Chinese state orphanages that showed baby girls deliberately being left to die of neglect. The tiny girl died. Oprah closes this show with a benediction: "God bless you. Here's proof that tiny Mei Ming's life mattered." Mei Ming, Oprah is suggesting, is one of many who have helped prod the world's conscience.

Presenting Suffering

This program illustrates Oprah's way of showing suffering and offering an explanation for this portrayal: Every life matters. Showing faces to raise awareness and to move people to action was part of Oprah's motivation for her 2002 trip to Africa. But suffering has to be presented in ways that don't lose an audience. If they don't tune in, there's no one to educate except an already informed choir. Oprah looks for universals; she emphasizes a common humanity rather than something happening on some remote continent to very different people. She says in the November 2004 issue of *O, The Oprah Magazine*: "When I went to Africa with Christmas gifts, my prime goal was to show African children as happy and responsive and loving so that people could see, 'Oh, these children are just like my children.' When people see children with distended bellies and flies on their eyes, they block it out and don't relate."

The poet T. S. Eliot wrote, "Human kind cannot bear very much reality." On Oprah's show, abuse may be the subject of a show, followed the next day by an entertainer. However morally laudable or pressing, unrelieved focus on abuse or mistreatment of women or AIDS in Africa or any of the world's pressing needs doesn't make for good ratings, either. Without good ratings the television platform Oprah needs to "get people to think about things a little differently" would vanish. She says in a show on "Appreciating Your Life" (November 21, 2001), referring to a previous program about women in Afghanistan, "I had said then that if you're a woman born in the United States, you're one of the luckiest women in the world, but, you know, those shows did dismal ratings. You all didn't watch. You were out shopping or whatever." Harpo Productions said in 2001 that shows featuring celebrities and psychologist Dr. Phil McGraw drew their top ratings.[3]

In an unpublished master's thesis, Illinois State University graduate student Mark T. Haynes studied Oprah's "Change Your Life TV" programs. During her 1998–1999 television season, Oprah used "Change Your Life TV" as the show's theme. The shows were explicitly intended to motivate people to make positive changes in their lives and regularly featured self-help experts and a daily segment called "Remembering Your Spirit," to inspire viewers or encourage them to reflect or meditate. Haynes found that watching "Change Your Life TV" did lead to positive changes in how viewers thought, felt, and acted. He also said that being entertained played a part in bringing about the change. "The nature of television is one of entertainment; therefore, the more enjoyable the therapeutic messages are to the television viewer the more receptive the viewer will be to the messages."[4]

Entertainment is needed to get many people to pay attention to a positive message. TV may change lives not in spite of its entertainment value but precisely because it entertains. In this way, entertainment becomes less of an indulgence or denial of the world's pain and more an activity that adds necessary balance.

TV shows memorable pictures and tells engaging stories. It can be used for good, ill, and/or making money. Oprah has acquired power and influence in part from being perceived as someone motivated by her intention to improve lives, even when she hasn't explicitly made that her goal. After almost twenty years of repeating the message, she no longer needs to dwell on it, but it still is communicated by shows that focus on abuse or other moral issues. Were tales of suffering a daily staple, Oprah's intention of moral uplift and encouragement would have a great deal of heavy lifting to do.

Variety and the range of interests are what fans say attracts them to Oprah. One day the show will present memorable news photos, the next day it will present Oprah's favorite things to buy, the next it will feature a talk with actors such as Matt Damon or Gwyneth Paltrow. All these topics have a place at Oprah's talk show table. She stretches imaginations by offering disparate and diverse subjects.

The October 6, 2004, show, "Around the World with Oprah," illustrates the range of interests that she balances in her distinctive blend of entertainment, information, and inspiration. The show focuses on thirty-year-old women around the world, with information from thirty different countries. Some countries are treated at relative length—Cuba, Mexico, Iraq, Kuwait—while others are glimpsed through thirty-second pieces spoken by women standing on location in different countries. Many of the women are well-off professionals, a few glamorous. Also shown is a woman writer in Iraq. She is not shown going shopping. Instead, she describes the popularity of Valium as a way for women to numb themselves to the dangers of daily life in a war-torn country where electricity cycles on and off daily and ensuring personal safety can be challenging. The show also presents Henriette, who survived the genocidal massacre of a million Tutsis, an ethnic minority, in the African nation of Rwanda in 1994. Henriette, who was raped repeatedly and who had sixteen members of her family murdered, now works as a tour guide for a memorial in her country about the massacre. Oprah says about Rwanda, "It was a holocaust going on and we didn't pay attention." Henriette appears in person on the show. Oprah greets her with a warm hug and presents her with an Angel Network scholarship for college. In a brief interview, Oprah expresses puzzlement about Henriette's resilience under such dire circumstances. "What still gives you joy?" she asks her guest. Henriette responds that her responsibilities and children had kept her alive and moved her beyond hopelessness. "On this day," she explains, "I'm very happy."

This show sweeps quickly around the globe, peeking at women and their varied conditions and activities. Shopping may be fun in Kuwait, but women don't have the right to vote, a fact which Oprah reiterates. A lawyer from Ethiopia says she thinks Americans don't care about the rest of the world. Asking her audience if they agree, Oprah suggests that lack of information rather than lack of concern is the case. So Oprah is providing the information in an "around the world with Oprah" show. She is a trusted guide teaching a variety of lessons that different cultures offer—some fun, some grim, all informative.

A common criticism of Oprah is that she isn't political enough. Feminist Gloria Steinem, among others, chided her for not asking tougher questions when she interviewed George Bush and Al Gore during the 2000 presidential campaign. The AIDS epidemic in Africa and the status of women in countries around the world have political reasons, causes, and repercussions. Oprah keeps her focus on individuals. For a woman who doesn't hesitate to recommend books and lots of her favorite things, Oprah shies from political recommendations. This is in keeping with her goal to appeal broadly. If she gets specific, she may lose some segment of her audience. This is true for religion as well as politics.

Yet it's also true that Oprah's work has helped to redefine what society considers social and public rather than individual and private. She has contributed mightily to opening the door on the issue of child sex abuse. Her concentration on what matters to women lifts these priorities into the public eye. Women's studies scholars say Oprah's work is consistent with the decades-long effort of the contemporary women's movement to make the personal political. Oprah has been clear that the secrets of abuse should be told outside the homes where it is happening so that suffering can be relieved and behavior changed. Some women scholars have applauded Oprah for advancing women's concerns in this way.[5] You are not alone with your problems, Oprah says. Suffering gives people a common lot.

Chapter Three

Oprah Provides Community

*W*hen I began watching Oprah in 2002, I talked to people whose job it is to teach or preach religion, or to think about how religion influences our culture. I asked them whether they could think of Oprah as a teacher who advanced a kind of entry-level religion that included the same core values many religions promote. One objection I heard is that Oprah's followers are not really a community the way an organized religious group is a community, providing a web of friendships and social ties, providing opportunities for one to talk and work with others, providing companionship that is both spiritual and social. "You're not going to be able to sustain a spiritual life with practices or virtues apart from communities of practice," says L. Gregory Jones, dean of Duke Divinity School.

Although Oprah brings tourists to Chicago, where the show is filmed, there is no Oprahtown or Cathedral of O where people can gather. Footage of Harpo Studios, where the program originates, is incorporated into the show, so the viewer does get some sense of being there. When I saw the building in person I was surprised at its modest size for the headquarters of a multimillion-dollar enterprise.

Yet a common interest contributes to an identification with a community of Oprah fans. Fans have something to talk about: today's or last week's show. Because Oprah has several media platforms—the show, the magazine, the Web site, the *After the Show* program on the Oxygen network—her influence and visibility extend well beyond the show's daily audience. Oprah is a person, an entertainer, a brand. It is possible to identify yourself as an Oprah fan by buying shirts, bags, caps, jackets, or pajamas bearing Oprah's distinctive logo. I have received two Oprah shirts as holiday gifts.

Oprah apparel can make a statement in public, like a bumper sticker or uniform. My brother-in-law told me of a time he shared a flight into Chicago with three women passengers whose shirts and loud conversation let him and others on the plane know they were Oprah fans and members of Oprah's Book Club.

Member of the Club

If community includes a sense of belonging to a group and the identity that gives you, whether you're a Baptist or a Beyonce fan, Oprah fans can and do experience community in Oprah's Book Club. When you buy an Oprah recommended book, you are participating in what Oprah describes as "the world's largest book club," with more than 460,000 members. That's a sizable community, with a shared vocabulary of books. Membership in Oprah's Book Club isn't like belonging to the Rotary Club, which meets regularly and engages in community work. But Oprah's books give you something to talk about in your own book club, or with your friends. Oprah's Web site also hosts virtual book discussions. Anyone carrying a book with the distinctive "Oprah's Book Club" logo has something in common with hundreds of thousands of others, since an Oprah recommendation multiplies sales dramatically. The club gives readers a common interest, common subject matter, common identity, however limited, in a pluralistic, media-drenched culture that offers lots of very different things to read and talk about. The members don't read just any books of the thousands published each year. They read Oprah's recommended novels. Oprah's picks have become what booksellers know as "hand sells"—recommendations that seem tailored to you and your interests from someone whose judgment you respect.

Beyond common subject matter, Oprah has specifically shaped her book club to encourage people to read and talk about books. She is a talk show host; talk is her specialty. On the surface, reading is a very different activity, which looks silent and solitary. On her TV show, however, Oprah draws a connection between reading and talking. The book club shows have included conversation among readers. In *Reading Oprah: How Oprah's Book Club Changed the Way America Reads*, author Cecilia Konchar Farr, an English professor, argues that the televised book club meetings presented on *The Oprah Winfrey Show* between 1996 and 2002 show the social nature of reading. A group of readers was invited to discuss their responses to a particular novel, sometimes in a dinner setting. Authors were present, but they were not authorities. Instead, the novel was the premise for conversation between readers. Farr says this way of understanding novels illustrates "the talking book."[1] The image of a "talking book" comes from early African American history, in which literacy meant being fully human in a country whose constitution held that black slaves counted as only three-fifths of a person. Slavery and education didn't go together. Novels are also for "talking about," Farr notes, quoting author Toni Morrison, who appeared four times on Oprah's Book Club shows to help guide readers.[2] A significant number of Oprah's picks were books by women of color, some with plots that referred to the larger societies in which the characters were situated. Many raised themes of social justice.

Book discussions are also the excuse for women to get together, as women's studies scholars have noted. They are the contemporary equivalent of nineteenth- and early-twentieth-century groups of "literary ladies." Farr writes, "By reading, and reading well together, book group members challenge one another to think differently, to think critically, and to connect, to build community."[3] Getting people to think differently, and using television to promote that kind of thinking, has been a goal for Oprah. In the book club conversations the program showed, readers were caught in the act of reflecting on what they had read, comparing their questions and reactions, and listening to one another's responses. It shouldn't have worked. Book club shows did draw lower ratings.[4] Yet the cultural prominence Oprah gained was immeasurable, not to mention the publicity.

The book club continues today, although changed from its original form. Oprah now selects classics, and the book club segments take less than the full broadcast hour. In addition, the book club is now primarily an online effort at Oprah's Web site. Want to know what Oprah thinks about *The Good Earth*? She answers readers' questions about Pearl Buck's novel in an online video. More than 3,400 messages were posted in eighteen months about John Steinbeck's *East of Eden*, the first novel picked by Oprah for her classics book club.

Virtual Community

Oprah likes to say that people want to feel validated or valued. Her Web site offers many avenues to participate in the Oprah community. Like the show, the Web site is a kind of meeting place—part beauty shop, coffee shop, or kitchen—where women go to talk during a family gathering. It is a place to share troubles, sound off, celebrate. People can talk to Oprah, or think they are talking to her. They are also talking with one another.

The Web site is a real repository of information and opportunity for those with specific interests and the time to investigate. Begun in 1998, the site takes advantage of the World Wide Web's ability to pigeonhole information, offer hyperlinked jumps, post comments, and present audio and video. It accommodates an online Oprah workshop. Any and all of these opportunities can draw in computer-enabled Oprah fans. They extend Oprah's reach well beyond the show and magazine and can field traffic worldwide and around the clock for fans who are sleepless in Seattle or Sydney. It is a busy and rich site. You can react to the show, use an online journal, search the site for information on a particular topic, subscribe to a number of newsletters. If you sign up, Oprah will come to your computer mailbox with a daily dose of inspiration or information you can use.

Message boards invite comment. TV show viewers can extend the day's experience by discussing and reacting to the day's show. They comment, snort, and raise virtual eyebrows. They post questions and receive answers; sometimes the same question is asked repeatedly about a particular product featured on the show. If a viewer has missed a detail, she can ask. Occasionally guests from the show post messages to the show's bulletin board that offer opportunities for comment. Controversial guests—Aaron Estes, a pastor who killed his wife; convicted murderer Scott Peterson's mistress Amber Frey; Amy Fisher, imprisoned for shooting her lover Joey Buttafuoco's wife—can prompt numerous and heated postings of opinions. More than 15,000 messages debated U.S. intervention in Iraq in a three-month period following a two-part show in early February 2003, "Should the U.S. Attack Iraq?" This cyberdiscussion doesn't offer face-to-face interaction, but it does offer opportunities to listen, express, obtain information, and respond. It can open the door for connections. Harpo Productions polices the site and enforces house rules, which include no soliciting or promotion of products. Posts can be removed or a friendly reminder issued about following rules. Hundreds of message boards cover other topics, including the magazine, all the book club picks from 1996 through 2002, and even recipes you can use or e-mail to an uninspired friend.

Another community opportunity distinct from message boards are O groups, some of which have attracted thousands of postings. Almost 2,500 groups include support groups for people recovering from or living with abuse or addiction; people wanting to find others in the same state or city; people wanting to tell ghost stories, talk politics, pets, or pounds; women supporting women. O groups are in English, but English-speaking Oprah fans from around the world are plugged in to various groups. From requests for recipes to prayers, spontaneity rules, sometimes rich in detail. Birthdays are celebrated, e-mail addresses are exchanged, advice is sought, daily activities written about and commented on, family news shared. Some active groups have lasted several years. I briefly joined a group that began in 2002 and exchanged thoughts with a number of women worldwide. The group was interactive, with people responding directly to one another in a public forum. Virtual interaction has led to telephone and face-to-face meetings for some. In response to my question about virtual relationships, one woman wrote that every kind of interaction, whether real or virtual, had some value.

Oprah's Web site also opens the door for viewers to be part of the show. A list of topics being worked on for the show offers an opportunity for viewers to participate. Videotapes are solicited, with instructions for avoiding lighting errors, and an address for mailing them in is provided. Stories are solicited via an e-mail form. Last-minute reservations for taping are also available through the Web site. Viewers are asked to explain their interest in or connection to a particular subject. (What are your questions for newly elected U.S. senator Barack Obama? Know someone who only wears black? Someone who is a real-life hero? Are you a fan of Destiny's Child or *Seinfeld* or *Desperate Housewives*?) In this way, fans provide Oprah with material for her shows as well as a potential audience that will be especially responsive to the subject. It is clear from shows that subjects have volunteered their stories, or their friends or neighbors have suggested them. Fans can meet their favorite stars; women can get makeovers or advice on relationships, decorating, and fashion; people with problems from clutter to kleptomania can confess them on television. Even if you're not selected, the door is open, the possibility exists that you may someday be on *The Oprah Winfrey Show* or at least in the audience.

Company's Coming

Scholars talk about how Oprah (and other television talk show hosts, though Oprah is the premier example) has changed what people talk about publicly and how they talk about it.[5] A generation ago, abuse happened behind closed doors; now it is talked about on television. Experts can give numbers to describe issues, but talk show guests drawn from ordinary life speak from their own experience. Personal experience makes guests authorities on a subject. What the average viewer thinks or experiences counts in some way. It gets heard. Pioneered by Phil Donahue, Oprah's town meeting format, with the host roaming through the audience, plainly signals the consideration and inclusion of audience views. From the guests on stage to the studio audience to viewers at home, the average "you" is democratically included in what Oprah does. This sense of inclusion of *your* experience has helped to form the bond between Oprah and her viewers.

Even though you are in your house alone or at your computer alone, Oprah's work tells you that you are not alone. Problems that you thought were yours alone are shared by others like you. Oprah is criticized for reducing social problems or inequities to matters of self-esteem, yet over the years she has not hesitated to look at issues. Topics during 1986, the first year of national syndication, included juveniles on death row, affirmative action, racial prejudice, and welfare. These were produced along with shows on women who love too much and marital problems. Oprah is and has been issue-oriented as part of her mix of self-improvement and social improvement.

Oprah tackles community questions but personalizes them by zeroing in on individuals involved or affected, a common journalistic technique that reflects her earliest training. "Live from Miami: A Wake-Up Call to America" on September 13, 1993, followed the killing of tourists in Miami. "Anti-Abortion Protesters" on September 12, 1988, followed antiabortion demonstrations at the 1988 Democratic National Convention. "Are Talk Shows Bad?" broadcast September 12–13, 1994, tackled the subject of "trash TV"—sensational talk shows. This show illustrates how Oprah relies on individual opinions; she interviews audience members about what they think. But she also considers TV talk shows as a social issue: Are they bad for society as a whole? In a society in which many things seem beyond individual control, the views of individuals add up to a larger picture—a community.

Not everyone is convinced that Oprah's way of drawing people in and letting them talk onstage and online constitutes valuable community. Virtual community only goes so far, says Jones at Duke Divinity School. "Virtual communities are wonderful supplements, but they're not substitutes," he says. "I can say anything anonymously, but when people have continuity with me over time they find out whether there's anything to those things I say."

Still, Oprah's warmth and realness speak to people. She gives you something to talk about, something to think about, something to sound off about. Some receive her into their homes as they might a guest. Sociologist Thompson says he became interested in Oprah because his seventy-eight-year-old mother is a fan. "The highlight of my mom's day," he says, "is watching Oprah and Dr. Phil."

"She becomes community," says Phyllis Tickle, author of *God-Talk in America.* "She becomes a visit every afternoon."

Chapter Four

Oprah Promotes Self-Examination

If the unexamined life is not worth living, as the philosopher Plato suggested long ago, then "living your best life" now requires self-examination. The apostle Paul also suggested questioning yourself as a way to live a better, more faithful life: "Examine yourselves to see whether you are living in the faith. Test yourselves" (2 Cor. 13:5). Looked at simply as soul-searching, the commonsense counsel to know yourself is a good way to produce decisions you can live with and avoid the question "What were you thinking?"

Oprah provides a number of suggestions for knowing oneself and makes them easy to follow. Journaling is a prominent one. *O, The Oprah Magazine* includes the regular feature "Something to Think About," a journal-like page that can be torn out and saved. It poses four or five questions and provides lines to write answers. The page itself has style, with a brightly colored decorative background as in a journal, which you don't have to buy since you've already bought the magazine. The journaling questions explore each month's theme (love, money, balance, enjoying yourself), which the magazine calls its mission. The short questions act like writing prompts, inviting an answer from you, the reader: "List the people you could tell most anything to." "What was your family's financial situation when you were growing up?" "Which of your beliefs are unshakable?" In this way the magazine offers as a monthly staple if not food for thought at least a snack. The questions are not intended to be merely rhetorical, nor will they produce deeply reflective essays. There is not enough room. Reflection is not a forced exercise but is available for anyone willing to take advantage of the opportunity. The simple page gives a nudge in the direction of self-awareness for those who might not normally reflect. Writing things down is a basic discipline for anyone who takes her thoughts seriously. That's why we take notes or make lists.

The magazine is not the only opportunity Oprah provides for reflection. The Web site offers an online journal and tips on getting started. You can maintain your own journal at the site or participate in one of five shared journals that are kept by multiple authors. One, a gratitude journal logging reflections on things for which writers are grateful, contains more than 25,000 entries.

The shared journal is paradoxical. Journaling is generally understood as an unburdening of private thoughts. The shared journals are kept in common in a forum available for everyone to read and write in. As with much of what Oprah is known for, this forum redefines what is considered private. Secrets posted online are halfway out in the open, since the writer is not necessarily identifiable but has revealed something. Those who take part in the shared journaling can experience companionship. Oprah promotes a feeling of being with others even if the journal writer sits alone at her computer.

Journaling is one technique for getting to know yourself, a time-honored suggestion that is encouraged in other ways at Oprah's Web site. A "Know Yourself" section within the site is like an online self-help book, free for the computer enabled. It provides information from "life coach" experts in personal growth, message boards that people can use to exchange ideas and express support, and several series of questions intended to promote introspection: What's your emotional style? What's your passion? What are your beliefs? The questions are clearly psychologically oriented, dealing with emotions and experience. Some of the questions include space for an answer that can be printed out, comparable to the magazine's "Something to Think About" feature. It is quasi-therapeutic and intended to be helpful—another way of carrying out Oprah's intention to help you live your best life.

Oprah has linked self-knowledge to better health and successful weight loss, describing it in various ways over time and over various diets. Some of her slogans get retired, as she explained in

1998 when introducing her "Change Your Life TV" programming. "Get with the Program" had been used for two years as a theme song for the show, and it was time for a change. "I think y'all should have got with the program," she said on the September 8, 1998, "Change Your Life TV" season premiere.

Personal Growth

Oprah herself lives the examined life. Her way of talking about this changes, but the underlying idea remains. Self-knowledge and personal change can be talked about psychologically or spiritually. In the April 2005 issue of her magazine, Oprah writes that everyone who needs to lose weight also needs to ask herself questions about why the weight is there and why diets have failed. The answer she offers here is lack of self-worth. No one will succeed in losing weight if her diet is missing "a spiritual and emotional component," Oprah writes. Her spiritual component includes her recognition of being God's child as well as her parents' daughter, she continues. Her language here uses a specific name for the divine, but she can write elsewhere more generally about good health as a result of being connected to "the Source of all Being." Her language shifts. Sometimes it is psychological and other times spiritual, sometimes it is specific and other times more general.

Oprah is obviously her own best visible example of self-awareness leading to personal growth. Her dieting travails, played out over the years in public, have served to make her very imperfect, very human. The route she has taken to weight loss emphasizes self-knowledge as much as it does habit and action. The idea of "emotional eating" that Oprah popularized is one way to talk about the need for self-knowledge that will help a dieter to lose and keep weight off. Recognizing what psychological need food is satisfying requires reflection. One forty-three-year-old woman who followed an Oprah diet and was featured on the television show in 2002 told me she used journaling to understand the reasons for her eating. That practice caused her new and deeper opportunities for looking inward, she said, ultimately producing more lasting contentment. Food remained an issue, but one she approached more intelligently.

Oprah is a general contractor for self-knowledge and self-help who relies on specialist subcontractors to help people look within. On her show and in her magazine, she regularly calls on experts in specific areas. Abuse, self-esteem problems, infidelity, and lying all get interpreted by expert guests on her show. A stable of regulars has changed over time. Psychologist Phillip McGraw—Dr. Phil—proved exceedingly popular. He, "life coach" Martha Beck, and financial adviser Suze Orman now have columns in Oprah's magazine. These are people qualified to give advice, and they are brought to you by Oprah. She can be the one-stop marketplace for advice on multiple aspects of busy women's lives.

Dr. Phil developed his following, which led to his own television show, through regular appearances on Oprah's show from 1998 to 2002. A clinical psychologist and consultant, McGraw won Oprah's confidence, and a berth on her show, after he helped her win a suit filed by Texas cattlemen, who had accused her of slandering beef on a 1996 show about mad cow disease. McGraw subsequently became her go-to psychology expert for shows about family and relationship issues as well as the never-ending quest to lose weight. Perceived by some as bullying or oversimplifying, others love his no-nonsense approach. His combination of aw-shucks and bluntness—"What's your payoff?" and "How's that working for you?" are among his rationale-puncturing questions—generated enough of a following for him to develop several best-selling books and ultimately his own show. One of his books, *Self Matters: Creating Your Life from the Inside Out*, offers a guide to creating your "authentic self" by doing a lot of self-homework: tests, quizzes, exercises designed to get you better acquainted with yourself. The psychologist's work comes down to the basic command: Know yourself.

"Know yourself" sounds like an activity for which a psychologist or at least a piece of paper, preferably bound in a nice journal, is required. But self-examination can also be a spiritual or religious process. Using techniques for developing awareness, self-examination can also produce spiritual growth.

Growing Awareness

The practice of *Examen of Consciousness* was developed by St. Ignatius, founder of the Jesuit religious order, as part of a set of Christian spiritual disciplines to promote greater awareness of God. The fifteen-minute process includes a review of the day's activities and an expression of gratitude to God for them. The day's review is intended to help you see your habits in everyday activities. The ultimate point of the Examen is to look for God in daily activities, to develop a practice of looking for God in order to increase awareness of God. Looking for something increases the odds you will find it.

An Examen can be done in writing. Journaling can be a technique for spiritual growth, but it can certainly have other goals. "Journaling is not necessarily either Catholic or Christian or Ignatian," says Daniel Flaherty, a Jesuit priest based in Chicago. "It's not even religious." Depending on whether you are in therapy or looking for God or trying to get better at your job, the questions you ask for reflection will change. But the process of reflection is a technique to learn and to repeat. "It's a practice to help people move in a certain direction," Flaherty says.

Oprah may not be trying to move people in the direction of greater awareness of God, but she is clearly interested in moving them in the direction of greater awareness and personal growth. Personal growth is roomy enough to include spiritual development. Many of Oprah's TV show guests have talked about the process of growth and change as a spiritual one.

On her show and in her columns in the magazine, Oprah has advocated the use of a gratitude journal to record things for which the writer is grateful. Keeping a gratitude journal promotes, almost forces, reflection on the subject at hand. Used by someone for religious or spiritual purposes, focus on gratitude can bring to mind the maker of daily gifts, Flaherty suggests. "You would be grateful to the Lord who gives you these gifts," he says.

Chapter Five

Oprah Teaches Gratitude

Gratitude is said to be a virtue, but I find it helpful to think of it as a practice. Unlike playing the piano, meditating, or playing sports, the practice of gratitude is easy and painless. You practice it each time you thank someone. This is a courtesy Oprah observes as a talk show host. She invariably thanks each guest for his or her appearance and always closes the show with her thanks. Since she has spoken with and interviewed thousands of very different people in her career, Oprah has gotten extensive daily practice in gratitude.

Gratitude is like a muscle that needs to be used often. Even if a feeling of gratitude isn't there, practice helps. Practice brings about the sentiment. "What we have to do is practice, and the feelings come afterward," says M. J. Ryan, author of *Attitudes of Gratitude: How to Give and Receive Joy Every Day of Your Life.*

In Oprah's gospel, gratitude is a recognition of abundance, an acknowledgment of blessings. There is more than enough to go around, and getting a portion of that kindles gratitude. Gratitude measures the distance between have-not and have, and is a reminder of the journey, one that Oprah's own life exemplifies. "I have been beyond blessed," she told *USA Today* in 2004, when she opened her nineteenth television season by giving away 276 cars. "Every time I pass the front of my house I sing 'Jesus Loves Me,' and the other day I remember I was jogging past—and now it's like a superstition—I had gotten past without saying it and went back, 'Jesus loves me! Jesus loves me!' "[1]

Oprah may have learned "Jesus Loves Me" in the church where she grew up. But a religious basis for gratitude for undeserved love and grace won't school those whom organized religion doesn't

29

reach. Ryan suggests that Oprah teaches some of what used to be learned in churches to people who don't necessarily have a formal religious practice or membership. "People receive the message from her that they couldn't get from anywhere else," Ryan says. The "nones"—Americans who say they have no religious affiliation—are a large, and growing, group, measured in a 2004 National Opinion Research Center study at 14 percent of the population.

Gratitude has been a repeated practice and subject on *The Oprah Winfrey Show*. Oprah has referred to the gratitude journal she keeps. In a gratitude journal, the writer lists five things each day to be grateful for. Keeping the journal provides daily practice. Oprah says she took the lesson of gratitude from the 1995 best-selling book *Simple Abundance* by Sarah ban Breathnach, who has appeared on a number of shows.

The April 17, 2000, show, "Gratitude Stories," opens with Oprah's words, "Thank you. Two words that can make miracles." Ban Breathnach is a guest, and a number of other guests whose stories are featured discuss gratitude journals. Husband and wife John and Karen Calvin talk about Karen's recovery from a car accident in 1982 that left her paralyzed from the neck down and feeling depressed and suicidal. But the husband's steady support brought his wife around. Karen says, "And I am so grateful to John for, once again, seeing in me what I didn't see in myself." Karen, a nurse, went on to found the National Spinal Cord Injury Hotline.

Later on the show, guests Jules and Jan Broom describe how their daughter Shannon inspired them through her gratitude journal, which they found and read after she was killed in an automobile accident. They used her art and words to make and give away 20,000 bookmarks, a process of "bookmark therapy" for their grief. Oprah wraps up the show by saying, "If you start being grateful for what you have, you will begin to see that you have more. That is how you increase abundance in your life, is by seeing what you already have."

On these as on other shows, life stories teach and testify. Like a preacher, Oprah asks for a witness and then presents guests who offer examples of how gratitude has benefited their lives. They function as encouraging role models of positive thinking, resilience, and gratitude.

Cope and Hope

The positive effects of gratitude and how gratitude helps people cope and heal from grief and loss were dramatically illustrated in shows Oprah did following the September 11, 2001, terrorist attacks. The November 21, 2001, show, "Appreciating Your Life," features guests whose lives were affected directly or indirectly by the terrorist attacks. Lyz Glick, who lost her husband on one of the hijacked planes, says, "I can either, you know, not embrace my life and live in the past of this tragedy of September 11, or I can look at things that I was thankful for in a relationship, you know? And I thank God that I did have, you know, five years of marriage." Other guests speak about making decisions based on a different sense of what really matters. One man tells Oprah of his plans to move to South Africa and volunteer at a school for the deaf.

Some of the language in this show veers close to religion without being too explicit. Oprah begins by invoking the words of the medieval Christian mystic Meister Eckhart: "If the only prayer you ever say in your life is thank you, that will be enough." She tells Glick that the family will be in her prayers. She jokes that she keeps a daily gratitude journal "religiously." She asks Glick about making a transition from a physical to a spiritual relationship with her husband. She urges viewers "for the love of all that is holy" not to waste time but to be grateful for time given.

Two days earlier, the show theme was "Thank You Day," and Oprah opens and closes this show too by referring to Meister Eckhart's words about gratitude. Several guests on this show had been affected by September 11. Sheila Moody, injured when a hijacked plane crashed into the Pentagon in Washington, DC, relates on videotape the story of her rescue by a cook in the building. Appearing in the studio, Sgt. Christopher Braman, the cook, tells the same story from his point of view. The two meet in front of the cameras, and Moody thanks her rescuer. In their stories, both Braman and Moody say they prayed for help.

"And at that point, I just said, 'Jesus, Jesus, you've got to help me,'" Moody says. Braman also recounts his prayer: "I said, 'Dear Lord, give me the strength for what I'm about to do.'"

Oprah appears struck by the details of the woman's story. She says to her, "You say, 'Jesus, Jesus,' and then he [Braman, the cook] shows up." Her implication is that the rescuer's appearance is no coincidence. References to Jesus aren't frequent by Oprah guests, but they do come up in some stories. They also come up in gospel music she occasionally presents.

"Counting blessings" has a religious sound. But it is used enough—by optimists, anyway—to qualify as a secular expression. "Oprah's Day before Thanksgiving Show," which aired November 24, 1993, presents some of the annoyances of the holiday—family fights, the challenges of holiday travel—but Oprah concludes her introduction with a reference to the meaning of Thanksgiving: "But we all know that Thanksgiving is really about counting your blessings—at least I hope we all know that." Guests will help her make that point. At the end of the show, she interviews several people who lost their homes in a fire a month earlier.

Beyond words and life stories that illustrate and model gratitude, Oprah includes opportunities for practice. Practice helps people learn skills and habits, and Oprah offers repetition and reinforcement for the teaching of gratitude. At her Web site you can send gratitude e-cards. The free cards feature quotes about gratitude. A "Thoughts for Today" section includes quotes organized by topic, and one of the topics is gratitude. You can keep an online journal at the site, either as a collectively shared journal, or as a private, individual one. Oprah closes the April 17, 2000, show, "Gratitude Stories," by steering people to these resources: "Here's a convenient way to do it. You can go to Oprah online now, and we have an online journal all set up."

Research on Gratitude

Psychologists Robert A. Emmons of the University of California, Davis, and Michael McCullough of the University of Miami have shown that people who keep gratitude journals are healthier, more optimistic, and more satisfied with their lives than those whose journals record neutral or problematic events. They have also found that people with gratitude lists are more likely to have progressed toward an important personal goal. Other researchers have found that gratitude is a coping strategy. People who are grateful can cope better with stressful life events. Gratitude also correlates with religiousness or spirituality. People who are more grateful tend to be less materialistic and more spiritual, regardless of whatever specific religion they practice. "A conscious focus on blessings may have emotional and interpersonal benefits," write Emmons and McCullough in a 2003 study.[2] They also say that gratitude is a response to moral behavior and a motivator of it. People who receive benefits are themselves likely to act to benefit others.

Oprah uses her other media and opportunities to push the practice of gratitude. The theme of the November 2000 issue of *O, The Oprah Magazine*, is gratitude, an obvious choice for the month of Thanksgiving. Oprah begins an interview with writer and Holocaust survivor Elie Wiesel with a question about gratitude:

> **Oprah:** There may be no better person than you to speak about living with gratitude. Despite all the tragedy you've witnessed, do you still have a place inside you for gratefulness?
>
> **Wiesel:** Absolutely. Right after the war, I went around telling people, "Thank you just for living, for being human." And to this day, the words that come most frequently from my lips are "Thank you." When a person doesn't have gratitude, something is missing in his or her humanity. A person can almost be defined by his or her attitude toward gratitude.

Another well-known writer's views on gratitude are discussed in the July-August 2000 magazine. Then First Lady Hillary Clinton writes that the work of Henri J. M. Nouwen, a popular Catholic writer about spirituality, taught her to count blessings. "I had never thought of gratitude as a habit or discipline before, and I discovered that it was immensely helpful to do so," Clinton writes.

In Oprah's gospel, these recurring references to gratitude are reminders. They serve to teach without preaching. Oprah remains open and curious about this virtue and can find plenty of stories that model it. She is occasionally prescriptive about it, telling viewers what to do in the imperative voice: "Above all, be grateful." But she is usually more verbally subtle, letting "gratitude goddess" ban Breathnach be more directive, or having the lesson flow from life stories she has presented.

Prayer as Practice

Prayer also gives practice in gratitude. A short article in the August 2004 issue of the magazine doesn't prescribe prayer or tell you to say grace before meals. Author Lauren F. Winner writes that saying grace transforms a meal into a celebration. You don't have to pray, but it will help you celebrate. The grateful person knows that she lives well. "Saying grace suggests not only the *grazie* of thanksgiving but also the calm, gracious elegance of living fully and well," Winner writes. Who doesn't want to live well, especially when it's only an acknowledgment of gratitude away? The "should" stick has been replaced by the "reward" carrot.

M. J. Ryan counts gratitude among what she calls modern virtues. Modern virtues—qualities of heart and mind including patience, kindness, gratitude, and generosity—can be cultivated, she says. Gratitude is noticing what's right and cultivating that recognition often and regularly. "Is it driving to work, saying something at the dinner table, keeping a journal? The trick is to find the one you will do."

Like many, I keep a gratitude journal. I got the idea for keeping one from Oprah. I began it in 2004 when I was taking part in a spiritual formation group. We were asked to pick a discipline, something we would do each day that would serve to remind us of things of the spirit. I chose a gratitude journal because it seemed easy and natural rather than something I would have to force myself to do. I have written in it virtually every day since. I write in it even when I don't feel particularly grateful. It has given me insight into discipline as well as gratitude. Consistency is more important than my feeling of gratitude, which may be present on any given day or not.

I have become grateful for the task. I have no sense of compulsion about the writing. It helps me not take things for granted, as so many guests on Oprah have affirmed from their experience. It shifts my focus to what has gone well, provided delight, or been a literal or figurative gift, sometimes long after I have received something. Along with scientists and Oprah guests, I have found the practice encourages satisfaction with what I have. Thanksgiving is less of an effort and more of a habit.

Chapter Six

Oprah Makes Things Simple

Amid all the goods she gives away or recommends, Oprah-style simplicity needs a little explaining.

It is definitely not the minimalist kind. She is more abundant than austere, a message her body has always telegraphed. With its ad-filled heft, lavish use of color, and slightly oversize dimensions, *O, The Oprah Magazine* also conveys the same image. Its editorial mission describes it as "a banquet of lush images, generous in scale and spirit." Amy Gross, editor in chief of the magazine, told *Mediaweek* she knew early on that a picture of a single flower in one stark and elegant vase just wasn't Oprah's style.[1] Tucked in the pages of the magazine is a regular feature called "Breathing Space." This two-page picture shows a vista from nature and a one- or two-sentence invitation to stop and relax. It provides a visual vacation.

Oprah believes in abundance, a concept not generally associated with religion. A lot of people think of religion as requiring asceticism and poverty—giving up goods, denying personal desires. And for good reason. Jesus told his followers to leave their families and give up their goods. The lives of the saints include plenty of ascetics. The Buddha's journey to enlightenment began with strict fasting.

Yet religious stories also show other ways. When Jesus was besieged by hungry followers, he whipped up a simple meal of loaves and fishes for them. Probably not mahi-mahi accompanied by saffron-rosemary brioche, but he did pull out the stops with quantities. There were twelve baskets of leftovers after he fed five thousand. His first miracle, at his mother's request, was to provide very good wine for guests at a wedding feast. Indeed, Jesus spent a lot of time eating with people, sometimes with dining companions so disreputable that he scandalized the religious authorities of the time. The Buddha realized he had gone too far with his asceticism, and after attaining enlightenment he taught a middle way. Some of his first followers were the monks with whom he had been fasting.

The point is that earthly goods have their uses and their delights. An ethic of simplicity can govern their use. Living simply does not mean living without stuff, but living wisely with it, unencumbered by it.

Here is where Oprah fits in. She is a guide who offers a list to help you choose lotions, potions, and fashions. The "O list," a regular feature in the magazine, includes an eclectic assortment of personal or household goods, from purses to pillows, in a variety of price ranges, some modest, some pricey. People who like her can use her opinion to decide what to pay for. Oprah is a clutter cutter, the winnower of goods and good causes: this handbag, that movie, this book, that social issue. At the beginning of her 2004–2005 television season, Oprah gave away 276 Pontiac G6s to audience members, many of whom needed a new car. The car's advertising manager said that the connection to Oprah helped distinguish the brand new model from other cars and other car advertising. "There's a lot of clutter out there right now," Mary Kubitsky said in the *Detroit Free Press*. "We had to find a way to break through."[2]

The value of an Oprah recommendation or connection is well known. Her holiday show "Oprah's Favorite Things" has become an annual cornucopia for her studio audience, evolving since 1996 from suggestions for holiday gift-giving into a giveaway bonanza in 2004 of $15,000 worth of products to each person in an audience filled with teachers. After a February 22, 2005, show about the secrets of looking ten years younger, a bulletin board discussion among viewers at the Web site honed in on a cream one guest said she used on her face, with the name of the cream repeatedly requested. Oprah's Book Club, which made best sellers out of her literary picks, is a visible and sustained example of her golden touch.

If you are skeptical about how simple this is, you are not alone. Some Oprah observers say that her gospel promotes a torrent of consumer goods, from pillows to candles to endless varieties of lipstick.[3] The cost of Oprah's "favorite things" can add up, and their presence can require dusting and/or closet space. "O's Golden Notebook" in the December 2004 magazine showcases gold-colored accessories that will decorate a home for the holidays. Among the "gracious, glamorous" items is a gold tassel costing $325.

Maybe better than most, though, Oprah presents herself as someone who recognizes the difference between a good thing and too much of it, knows the divide between being voluptuous and being fat. Oprah's gospel is a material one that has its limits. Excess eventually piles up into household clutter, which then is another problem to be solved. The November 18, 2004, show "How Clean Is Your House?" starts out as a housecleaning exposé, featuring a woman who describes her own home, filled with pet poop and rotting food, as excessively dirty. The show then goes on to present information about compulsive hoarding as the "dirty secret" of a million Americans. As usual for shows dealing with problems and dysfunctions, an expert was featured, with additional online information pointed to. "Clutter buddys" are among the support groups that you can join at the Web site. Oprah made the cleaning of her own closet into both a show, broadcast November 9, 2004, and a charity event. She dubbed the wardrobe slenderizing and organizing "visual therapy" and urged viewers to clean out their own closets. Harpo staffers bought the closet culls, and gowns were auctioned off to the studio audience, raising at least $40,000 for Oprah's Angel Network, her public charity.

The "Shop Like a Genius!" guide in the September 2004 issue of the magazine, which at 334 pages is chock full of ads, contains some interesting recommendations and advice. In "What I Know for Sure," the regular column by Oprah that concludes each issue, Oprah recounts an experience at an antiques store. She was admiring an eighteenth-century cherry dressing table but told the salesman she had no real need for it. He in turn told her that his wares were not there because people need them, but because they enjoy them. It was an "Aha!" moment for Oprah. "Some things are to be treasured and enjoyed," she writes. She doesn't say whether she bought the table, but goes on: "You enjoy everything a lot more when you're not overreaching." It's characteristically written from Oprah's experience, which ranges financially, she explains, from living in debt to being able to buy "anything, *anything*." Not many people have the experience of being able to buy anything, but many can relate to indebtedness. The message of the column is its headline: "I still think twice before I buy anything." That's the advice Oprah wants readers to follow, not "Deny and don't buy."

In case you need some coaching on how to think about buying, "Something to Think About," the magazine's regular two-page feature that poses questions for reflection and provides space to answer them, asks you to consider how you could be a more discriminating shopper. It doesn't advocate producing many journal pages or spending hours soul searching. It just asks a few questions. The article "The End of Nothing-to-Wear" advocates surprisingly few pieces of clothing for closet essentials: two pairs of pants, three skirts, one dress. Outfits illustrating fall clothing trends are shown in three versions: higher, medium, and lower-end prices. Her magazine typically features goods in a number of price ranges. Reader incomes likewise show a spread. More than a third of the magazine's readers have household incomes under $50,000; more than one-quarter have household incomes over $100,000. Oprah may be paying homage to shopping, but she's not encouraging indebtedness.

You can also give it away as well as spend it on yourself. Oprah certainly does both. The mission—that is, the magazine's theme—for the March 2005 issue is money: how to manage, save, and give it away. Special Olympics CEO Timothy Shriver writes, "A big part of how to spend is how to give." "O to go," the tear-out feature in each month's magazine that gives the reader something to use, such as a bookmark or postcard, consists of eight coupons with amounts ranging between $10 to $150. Each coupon names a charity and specifies what a donation to that charity will fund: $75 buys a sewing machine for a Rwandan woman, $10 provides

HIV/AIDS education in Africa. It's easy: tear out the coupon, write a check. The charity's address is right on the coupon, making a response effortless.

Cut through the Glut

Besides advocating some middle way in the possession of material stuff, there is a second way in which Oprah keeps things simple. She declutters information, as the charity coupons illustrate. She pares it down to select statistics, memorable phrases, short summaries. This is most clearly seen in her use of television time, where time is money and needs to smoothly incorporate interruption for advertisements. She uses the medium as a laser on information, editing and packaging details and stories. TV is a medium that doesn't lend itself to conveying complex information: numbers, nuances, on the other hands, and yes-buts. When *The Oprah Winfrey Show* presents a story, whether a story of a guest or information about an issue, the presentation is highly visual, highly personalized, and highly edited. Oprah has mastered the efficient use of chunks of time. Shows in the 1980s and early 1990s, when the format was participatory and Oprah stood in the audience fielding comments and questions, sometimes ended with Oprah's announcing, "Show's over," or cutting off a speaker. She closed a September 12, 1988, show on antiabortion protesters by saying, "This has nothing to do with anything, but Happy Rosh Hashanah." By contrast, an hour-long show about women around the world broadcast October 6, 2004, took readers to thirty countries and accommodated seven commercial breaks. That's one whirlwind tour from the armchair.

Like any other source of information in the culture, Oprah is an information gatekeeper. What gets through the gate to her viewers is information anchored in fact and colored with emotion, to move people to thought—to think a little differently about things, as Oprah puts it—or to action. Oprah uses a simple, concrete vocabulary and subject matter. Shows about issues—AIDS in Africa, women in Congo, abusers—offer follow-up, resources, groups, additional information at the Web site. Viewers can do something if they are inclined.

Oprah is famous for being nonjudgmental, but she will offer guidance, sometimes advocating very specific action. "Now that you have heard, you can't pretend you didn't hear it," she said at the conclusion of a January 24, 2005, show about the rape of women in Congo. "You need to see *Hotel Rwanda*," Oprah said very prescriptively. (*Hotel Rwanda* is the 2004 film about a hotel keeper who saved the lives of more than a thousand people during the 1994 genocide in that country. The conflict spilled soldiers into the neighboring nation of Congo.) One of the guests, Zainab Salbi, represented Women for Women International, a human rights organization fostering greater awareness of global women's needs. Oprah's viewers were asked to do something easy: to write letters through Women for Women International to another woman in Congo. They weren't asked to join peacekeeping forces in Africa. Oprah advocates global consciousness, but she scales things down—to letter writing, to community volunteering—so they are doable. She is interested in providing women with a set of instructions, a "how-to." She would call it empowering. That helps to avoid that feeling of frustration and powerlessness in a world where many claims are made on compassion.

Presenting Issues

Oprah makes a point of not being explicitly political. Nor is she partisan. On September 11, 2000, Oprah opened her television season by interviewing Democratic presidential candidate Al Gore. Eight days later, she interviewed Republican presidential candidate George W. Bush. That equal-time approach resembled a League of Women Voters–style candidates forum. In the 2004 presidential election Oprah's recommendation was simply to vote. On a September 29, 2004, show that also provided the occasion for registering audience members to vote, she reached out to women, telling them they could make a difference. Instead of presenting numbers in the millions or recapping candidates' stands on issues, she picked a few, small-scale details. She focused on the 537-vote margin in the state of Florida that helped to give the 2000 presidential election to Bush. She singled out an African American audience member who admitted she was not registered to vote and told her, "You as an African American woman understand the price that was paid." On a follow-up show on November 3, the day after the 2004 presidential election, the woman told Oprah and viewers that she had registered and voted.

Oprah is clearly interested in informing her audience of women about topics that affect political policy, such as AIDS, Africa, and international women's issues. But she shies away from the abstract language of "issues." The April 2003 issue of the magazine includes a story about her trip to South Africa in 2002. She describes it as a Christmas gift for herself, writing, "I wasn't trying to eradicate AIDS, end poverty, or stimulate economic development. I simply wanted to create one day that the kids could remember as happy." This is easier to depict for her viewers and easier to do.

Her goal is stated in modest terms: Make some children happy. It is not very abstract, nor is it as tall an order as ending poverty in South Africa. But almost anyone can make a child happy for at least one day. In Oprah's case, she has the resources to make 50,000 children happy. But that scope isn't required in order to make a difference. The essential task is human-sized: Throw a celebration, give out gifts. Creating a day that children would remember is a concrete action to better children's lives, one of Oprah's career-long missions.

"I don't think she's sat down and done scientific and social and political analysis of the system," says Jamie T. Phelps, a theology professor and director of the Institute for Black Catholic Studies at Xavier University of Louisiana. "The beauty of what she's doing is that simple people—and that's the majority of us—can understand."

Want to lose weight? Take ten thousand steps a day, starting with one. Want to unstick a relationship that disappoints? Repeat the phrase, "He's just not that into you." (Blunt but not abrasive, these mantralike words are the subject of the bestselling relationship guide *He's Just Not That into You*, as well as a September 22,

2004, show.) Honesty is distilled into a memorable mantra and call to awareness.

Developing the virtue of gratitude is a bit more of an abstract effort, but Oprah tries to translate it into a doable simple practice. For several years, she advocated and spoke about her use of a gratitude journal. At the close of the April 17, 2000, show, "Gratitude Stories," she reminds viewers about practicing gratitude and guides them to a means to do it. "Here's a convenient way to do it. You can go to Oprah online now, and we have an online journal all set up." Developing gratitude and awareness by seeing what you already have makes sense for the philosophically inclined. Others need to make a little list of five specific things. Putting pen or keystroke to paper is something simple that anyone can do.

Oprah's simple communication has been belittled as fortune cookie wisdom and lightweight pop psychology. But dismissing it doesn't really explain its appeal. Linguist Deborah Tannen, whose best-known book *You Just Don't Understand: Women and Men in Conversation* looks at the differences between how men and women talk, has said that Oprah has understood that television can be used to communicate as a family member would. "She makes people care because she cares," writes Tannen.[4] Blending the walk with the talk, she uses TV to *show* she cares. She also uses the simplicity it requires to keep her own message short enough to remember. The best teachers, including spiritual teachers, also do that. The Buddha made lists: the Four Noble Truths, the Eightfold Path. Moses received only ten commandments. In Islam, God has ninety-nine names, a challenging but finite list. Keep it simple.

In his small but influential work *A Testament of Devotion,* twentieth-century Quaker writer Thomas Kelly talks of simplicity as the fruit of obedience to the will of God. Attuned to that will, simplicity is effortless. You can have a busy day and still remain in God's presence, praying while working. What Kelly calls a "singleness of eye" amounts to inner simplicity—a simplicity of spirit—that coexists with outer duties such as job, family, volunteer work. It coexists with goods, understanding that they are resources to be rightly used and delights to be enjoyed. Inner simplicity lies in doing what God wants. No desires or goods get in the way of doing that.

Many religions talk about surrendering to the will of God. Islam is founded on that; *Islam* literally means "submission." While visiting a Baptist church in Ohio, Oprah told members of the congregation to "surrender all," invoking the words and theme of the hymn "I Surrender All," a song she has found meaningful.[5] The writer of the hymn, Judson W. Van De Venter, wrote the song at the turn of the twentieth century as he struggled with a career question: whether to pursue art or evangelism. He gave up visual art, but became a composer of hymns. He surrendered his desire, but not his creativity. Oprah chose TV. She might even say God chose TV for her, and she surrendered.

Chapter Seven

Oprah Listens

> For the confessions of my past sins (which thou hast "forgiven
> and covered" that thou mightest make me blessed in thee, trans-
> forming my soul by faith and thy sacrament), when *they* are read
> and heard, may stir up the heart so that it will stop dozing along
> in despair, saying, "I cannot"; but will instead awake in the love
> of thy mercy and the sweetness of thy grace, by which he that is
> weak is strong, provided he is made conscious of his own weak-
> ness. And it will please those who are good to hear about the past
> errors of those who are now freed from them.
>
> —Augustine, *Confessions*

*D*espite his rather formal language, Augustine would make a great
talk show guest. His *Confessions* stands as a fourth-century mem-
oir of his life makeover through God's spiritual fitness program.
Augustine says that confession is therapeutic. It alleviates depres-
sion and empowers the weak. Hearing about "past errors"—Augustine was probably a party animal before his repentance and
makeover—is also helpful to others. Confessing and listening
strengthen the person who confesses, as well as his or her listeners.

The Oprah Winfrey Show is renowned as a place of confession.
Oprah talks about her own "past errors," guests tell their life stories
to inspire or to offer cautionary tales. Fans say they appreciate that
Oprah is an open, nonjudgmental listener as she hears from a wide
range of guests. Her interview subjects have ranged from ex-
presidents to ex-prostitutes, from convicted child molesters to such
moral heroes as South African archbishop Desmond Tutu. Oprah's
guests have confessed pedophilia, rape, murder, infidelity, addic-
tions, physical abuse, and all manner of crimes and misdemeanors.

The October 1, 2004, show, "I Shot My Molester," illustrates Oprah's mix of materials and guests to get her point across. Real-life stories from two guests are shown, then the show shifts to promote the movie *Woman Thou Art Loosed*, based on a novel by popular preacher Bishop T. D. Jakes, who drew the material for the novel from his experience counseling abused women. Jakes also plays himself in the film. "How does coming forward help the women?" Oprah asks the pastor in her interview. Finding out you're not in isolation helps, says Jakes, who, like Oprah, turned experience into a cautionary tale.

Telling

Secrets are told for a number of reasons—to confess to doing wrong, to unveil a wrong done, to repair a harm, to seek help with a hidden problem. On the show "Confronting Family Secrets," which aired November 12, 2003, a man who acknowledged molesting his sister, a filmmaker, tells why he agreed to participate in a documentary she made about her abuse. "I decided that by not speaking that I would be contributing to the culture of silence that—that pervades this issue, and that is wrong. That needs to be addressed," he says. "Nothing changes in America until it is spoken about," says Jakes on the October 21, 2004, show, "Sexually Abused Women Come Forward."

The September 21, 2004, show, "Secret Lives," features two gamblers and one shoplifter, all women, and Terry Schulman, a former shoplifter who is now a therapist working with shoplifters. On the show, Oprah can play devil's advocate, posing questions that a skeptical person might ask—"I don't understand why this is an addiction"—and eliciting information that others in similar circumstances could use to face their secrets. Two guests say they wanted their stories to serve as cautionary tales. "I want to get the message out that you don't have to live in shame and secrecy," says Alice, a shoplifter. "If you're involved in something like this, reach out and tell someone," says Anne, who had embezzled from the Catholic high school where she worked in order to support her gambling habit. Secrecy harms the one harboring the secret, as well as those directly harmed by the behavior. Fear of being found out, a need for dishonesty that becomes chronic, and shame compound the original wrong. Keeping something secret also makes it impossible to repair harm. Disclosure is a step toward changing the situation for the better for wronged and wrongdoer.

On this topic, as on others, Oprah's Web site provides additional information and resources to deal with problem gambling and shoplifting. Contact information for national organizations dealing with problem gambling and shoplifting is listed. A message board provides an opportunity to discuss and confess secrets. Dozens of posters confess secrets or problems, asking for opinions or help and thereby constructing an e-community of those interested in the subject. Some have posted their e-mail addresses, making themselves available for correspondence. Others have posted messages revealing how they dealt with their own problems and offering advice and encouragement. A link leads to an online support group for addicts elsewhere at the Web site.

Besides opening an avenue for help, confession unburdens the soul. In the June 2002 *O, The Oprah Magazine*, author Francine Prose writes, "I was in the third grade when I first discovered the way that coming clean could make the soul feel freshly laundered." The evocative words echo scriptural language about purification: "Purge me with hyssop, and I shall be clean; wash me, and I shall be whiter than snow" (Ps. 51: 7). Catholics put this psychological dynamic to work in the sacrament of penance, commonly called confession.

The "mission"—the unifying theme—of the June 2002 magazine is "true confessions." In "Here We Go," a preface that introduces each month's themed articles, the woman who has heard thousands of televised confessions writes, "While a certain freedom can come with public revelation, I've learned that the most important confession anyone can make is not on TV or in the limelight. It's in those quiet, private moments when we all take on one of the most difficult challenges—confessing the truth to ourselves." The feature "Something to Think About"—which includes provocative questions intended to prompt self-reflection, on a page that can be torn out and saved—begins: "Think of confession as life's strategic opening move. It clears the air, draws you closer to others, frees up creative thinking, leads to inner peace."

The "O Calendar" for the month, another regular feature, is filled with quotes about confession ("True confession consists in telling our deed in such a way that our soul is changed in the telling of it," from Maude Petre, an English Catholic writer of the early twentieth century) and suggested activities ("Schedule regular times for unburdening with a spiritual advisor, counselor, therapist, or trusted friend"). A series of stories on aspects of confession include life coach Martha Beck's advice on when, what, and to whom to confess. "Perhaps our secrets struggle to be revealed because they know that confession can perform a miracle. . . . It can turn our worst mistakes or tragedies into beacons of hope for others," Beck writes. In another article, after an argument with her husband, writer Winifred Gallagher interviews four professionals—three clergy and a research psychologist—and her own mother, married for fifty-six years, about confession and contrition. Gallagher concludes, "Confession reconciles us to the fact that this is not a perfect world and we are not perfect people. . . . I was moved by the sacred imperatives of forgiveness and reform and by the notion that something good can come from our misdeeds."

Hearing

The act of telling requires a listener. "Practice open listening," advises the June 2002 "O Calendar." Confession is good for the soul in part for the acceptance that it can offer. It means being heard. Psychotherapy is effective when it provides catharsis—a clear sense of emotional relief from a burden, deliverance triggered by disclosure. "Coming forward releases something, does it not?" Oprah asks pointedly on the October 21, 2004, show, "Sexually Abused Women Come Forward." On that show she interviews three sisters who were all molested by their father, a Methodist minister. She also suggests a reason for keeping secrets:

Have you kept this secret because you were afraid of rejection, of not being loved? These are simple words, easy to relate to, easy to assent to.

Empathy and listening confer a kind of power on the listener even while the listener extends something to the speaker, namely, a sense of being heard. In the October 6, 1998, show, "Working with Emotional Intelligence," guest Daniel Goleman, author of the best-selling book *Emotional Intelligence*, tells Oprah that people want to be heard and understood. Oprah says they want to be validated. "And for years, when people would say to me, 'Why do you think people come on TV and tell the most unbelievable—' it's because nobody ever listened to them," Oprah tells him and viewers.

Listening has power. It is a mark of respect and acknowledges someone's existence and experience. Oprah talked about her fundamental belief while accepting the first-ever Bob Hope Humanitarian Award at the 2002 Prime-Time Emmy Awards. "The greatest pain in life is to be invisible," she said. "What I've learned is that we all just want to be heard. And I thank all the people who continue to let me hear your stories, and by sharing your stories, you let other people see themselves and, for a moment, glimpse the power to change and the power to triumph."

Listening and confessing have both psychological and moral meaning, and Oprah has presented both approaches. If "remembering your spirit" took a spiritual and empathetic approach, Dr. Phil the psychologist listened—but only up to a point before dispensing advice. The no-nonsense psychologist, who now has his own syndicated TV show, began on Oprah's show in 1998 as part of her change-your-life mission. McGraw's gruff, focused manner was intended to solve problems quickly, to pull out the weed of dysfunctional behavior rather than to ruminate about how deeply it might be planted or why it got there. McGraw's solutions needed to fit within an hour-long show or a magazine column, but not all his answers took less than one hour. His "Get Real Challenge," in which he worked with a group of participants seeking to change behavior they were unhappy about, was shown periodically throughout the 2001–2002 season.

Not Judging

Oprah is famously nonjudgmental and empathetic. She says, "I try to live in the place of no judgment" or "I'm not judging you" often enough to make it a touchstone of who she is. She says this to encourage her guests to open up and talk about shameful, difficult, or repugnant things. "Before you judge," says Oprah to viewers and audience on the September 21, 2004, show, "Secret Lives," "you just never know what's going on in other people's lives." To bring home her point at the show's beginning, Oprah reads responses that audience members have written to questions about what secrets they were keeping. "Nine women are having affairs," she said, reading from a list of transgressions audience members have anonymously disclosed. So what are you hiding? is the implied request. Know yourself. Implied also could be the famous advice from Jesus: "Do not judge, so that you may not be judged. For with the judgment you make you will be judged, and the measure you give will be the measure you get" (Matt. 7:1–2). Go ahead and hurl that stone, if you dare.

At the same time, Oprah is steering the audience to the place of nonjudgment. She speaks for the audience, which represents public opinion. She may anticipate or voice a judgment her audience might make, ask questions they might have about a behavior. But she also shapes her viewers' views.

Oprah is hardly alone in this softening of strict judgment. Oprahfication or not, it's easy to find. Alan Wolfe, author of *The Transformation of American Religion: How We Actually Live Our Faith*, contends that nonjudgmentalism pervades much of religion in this country today. Contrary to the stereotypical view of religion as sternly judgmental, he argues persuasively that religion's idea of sin has been replaced by the idea of a nurturing God—"God lite"—who will understand, accept, and ultimately forgive all.[1] Just as Oprah does, such a God listens—*really* listens.

Yet Oprah's generally nonjudgmental stance can disappear, notably when she interviews abusers. "What the hell does that mean?" she snorts skeptically when interviewing a man convicted of molesting his stepdaughter, who appeared with him on the

October 1, 2004, show, "I Shot My Molester." Nor did she follow her practice of greeting him; she did not shake the convicted abuser's hand. On the February 18, 2005, show, "Spouses Who Kill," she tells a pastor convicted of murdering his wife as he explains his version of what happened, "You're going to have to do better than that" and "What I really have a problem accepting is the selective amnesia." She says on the February 19, 1988, show, "Family Interbreeding," to a man who conceived children with three of his own daughters, "Do you understand that you're a slime?" That's judgment.

Healing

Talking and listening, disclosing and being heard, are part of healing, a function that religion too has played. The balm dispensed on talk shows is psychological, but it can act on a troubled soul. Confessing and being heard are necessary in order to heal from trauma. Interviewing actress Tracey Gold on the April 10, 2005, show, "Tracey Gold Convicted of Drunk Driving," Oprah asks her about the humiliation of publicly discussing a drunken driving accident that injured members of her family. "I would think this is going to be cathartic," Oprah says.

In that instance, confession deals with a wrong done and acknowledgment of it—or "owning it," a phrase popularized by Oprah's Dr. Phil. At other times it is about being wronged. Oprah has opened the household door on abuse. She has made the subject of child sexual abuse a personal and professional crusade from almost the very beginning of her television talk show career, a conviction rooted in her own experience. On the November 10, 1986, show, "Sexual Abuse in Families," broadcast just two months after her talk show began running nationally, she says, "I speak from personal experience because I was raped by a relative. . . . I am telling you about myself so that maybe the closet where so many sexual abuse victims and their molesters hide might swing open just a crack today and let some light in. Because it is in the light that some of life's worst problems can be examined and solved."

She concludes this show, in which she interviews three women who were molested, two fathers who molested their daughters, two therapists and an author, by again referring to her own experience: "I've healed very well, and just being able to say it to somebody begins the healing process." She goes on to provide a phone number that adults who were sexually abused as children can call for help and information.

Oprah has returned repeatedly to this subject throughout her work, with different aspects of the subject being explored: Can sex offenders be rehabilitated? Would you know if your child were being abused? What if you discover your husband is a molester? Oprah has also featured well-known, and sometimes less well-known, stories of child abduction and abuse, spotlighting them in order to press for resolution or attention or change. In 1991, the murder of four-year-old Angelica Mena of Chicago by a convicted child sex offender prompted Oprah to hire former Illinois governor James R. Thompson to draft legislation to create a national database of child abusers. Oprah testified and campaigned for its passage. President Bill Clinton cited her as an influence when he signed the National Child Protection Act of 1993, which established the database.

Molestation, whether by family members or an unrelated predator, is talked about openly in order to do something positive for victims who tell their stories—Oprah and many other antiabuse activists call it healing—or to prevent it from happening in the first place. Over years and dozens of shows about child molestation or abuse, the emphasis on prevention has grown. On the May 20, 2004, show, "The Mistake I Can't Take Back," Oprah interviews a fifteen-year-old girl who had been seduced by her softball coach, and the girl's parents. The focus was less on the teenaged victim and more on what the parents weren't seeing or didn't do or didn't suspect. As is always the case with Oprah, there is a lesson here. "That is the message of your mistakes," she says. "Child molesters are people we know." Oprah invariably thanks those who tell the stories of their victimization and calls them courageous.

Public Accounting

Oprah has been criticized for psychologizing problems and thereby absolving people of personal responsibility for crimes or bad choices. In the 1990s critics decried the "Oprahfication" of wrongdoing.[2] In this view, listening empathetically amounts to leniency. But Oprah's listening can also be seen as part of a public accounting of wrong that calls to account private rationalizations, bringing excuses out on stage. This is not a courtroom show, but you can be the judge at home. Once someone is on TV, there is no going back. Hearing and airing all does not necessarily excuse all.

The subject of "Live from Miami: A Wake-Up Call to America" on September 13, 1993, was the series of murders of foreign tourists in Miami that year. A total of twelve were killed in separate incidents. On this show, filmed in Miami, Oprah interviews a tourist who was assaulted but survived, officials and residents, the family of a victim, and the mothers of two arrested suspects. The conversation with the two mothers—Cathey Hazelhurst and Vera Hood—is very open.

> **Oprah:** I imagine as a parent it's one of the hardest things in the world to do, Cathey, to admit that your son is guilty of such a—such a horrible thing. But at least you admit it.
>
> **Cathey:** Of course . . .
>
> **Oprah:** . . . What we're trying to understand is, if your daughter has said she did it . . . why not just accept responsibility and let it . . .
>
> **Vera:** It's not like that. This lady says she loves her son and I love my daughter. But if my daughter did it, she should be punished for it. That's all I got to say.

At the conclusion of the show, Oprah calls the Miami situation a "wake-up call," a term she often uses. The show should wake up not only Miami citizens but those living in other communities and confronting the crimes that plague them. Information is intended to lead to some action. Families live in communities, as this show makes clear. The children of these mothers have affected the lives of other families, other community members. Oprah is not offering policy recommendations, but she can put a face on viewpoints and show that many are involved. This show includes all those sometimes conflicting views. Oprah's town-meeting-style format for her early shows lends itself to the multiple viewpoints and their airing and hearing. All those Oprah interviewed on this show have a stake in, and some responsibility for, public safety.

The Monkey in the Freezer

For all the accusations of egomania that have been made about a powerful and wealthy woman whose face is on every one of her magazine covers, Oprah has regularly held herself accountable for mistakes and bad judgments. She very publicly turned away from "trash TV" in the mid-1990s. The September 13–14, 1994, two-part show, "Are Talk Shows Bad?" tackled head-on the question of the social harm done by sensational talk shows. Oprah had as guest Vicki Abt, author of a study criticizing the harmful effects of talk shows. Toward the end of the second show, Oprah included an excerpt of a July 13, 1994, show, "Womb Regression," which featured a guest who said that his difficulty emerging from the womb affected his whole life thereafter. "Shame on me. Shame on me for that," Oprah says to psychologist Abt and viewers.

Oprah was conspicuous in her turning away from "trash TV." On the season premiere of the 1998–1999 "Change Your Life TV" season, with its conscious "moral uplift," Oprah advises actress Roseanne Barr, about to inaugurate her own talk show, not to invite such extremists as Nazis or Ku Klux Klan members, "because it gives them a platform." She regularly tells viewers now that shows featuring painful personal stories are not done for voyeuristic purposes. She jokes about public opinion regarding her relationship with longtime boyfriend Stedman Graham. She hears what the public is saying about her, whether in the form of ratings or of judgments.

"I think she has been very responsible in how she has gauged and monitored and disciplined her own actions in terms of her own principles," says Phyllis Tickle, former religion editor for the industry magazine *Publishers Weekly* and author of *God-Talk in America*. "She uses criticism and values her critics."

Oprah has also wrung humor from some of her choices. February 26, 1999's "Our Most Forgettable Shows" twits shows that have featured frozen monkeys, the best way to unroll toilet paper, kooky guests, and the proper color for your urine.

Far from dispensing with moral judgment, Oprah's ability to present and listen to a very wide range of guests and topics engages that judgment. Sociologist Eva Illouz says that the openness of Oprah's show—its commercial nature and its appeal to a large and diverse following—"enlarge[s] the scope of our moral imagination."[3] Oprah's universe is inclusive and pluralistic; many points of view can be considered, and all of them contribute something of value to a cultural conversation that includes many voices. The voices of ordinary people faced with extraordinary or demanding situations such as the loss of a loved one have an opportunity to be heard on Oprah's show, and the value of being heard is both social and psychological. It is also religious, for religions teach the value of confessing sins, affirming beliefs, and being publicly accountable.

Chapter Eight

Oprah Teaches Generosity

*O*prah's generosity may be the characteristic that her fans cite most frequently. Giving is a consistent theme of her shows, her magazine, and her Web site. Donating and volunteering are encouraged; people who "use their lives" by doing something socially worthwhile are often profiled. She walks her own talk. Oprah is a big donor and promoter of social causes, especially those related to families and education. It adds up to a highly visible model of generosity. If your checkbook won't let you match her amount, at least follow her example.

You don't even have to give till it hurts. Giving pays you back, by making the donor feel the joy of giving. The December 22, 2003, "Christmas Kindness" show about Oprah's trip to South Africa is classic Oprah, a demonstration of how she makes giving seem attractive and satisfying. She opens this show, which uncharacteristically does not include a live audience, with a story from her own life. When she was twelve years old, living with her mother in Milwaukee and on welfare, her mother decreed there would be no Christmas gifts that year, since there was no money. Three nuns visited the household, however, and brought Oprah a doll. That, she declares, made it a truly memorable Christmas. To repay their kindness years later, Oprah explains, she decided that she would sponsor a memorable Christmas for South African children.

South Africa is a deliberate and dramatic choice. Over scenes of a verdant countryside, Oprah says she felt as if coming home. South Africa is also one of the countries hardest hit by AIDS, which has killed millions and left more than two million orphans. "I knew we couldn't fix all that is wrong here," she says. But the gifts were intended to give children a sense of being cared about, as she had experienced herself as a girl in a difficult situation. "I wanted the children of South Africa to know they are remembered," she says. The trip was funded by her private charity, the Oprah Winfrey Foundation, and arranged in partnership with the Nelson Mandela Foundation.

Seeing the preparation for the trip builds anticipation as the viewer looks over Oprah's shoulder as she chooses gifts for children and teens, including backpacks, school supplies and books, dolls, candy, and shoes. This lesson has a little footnote: The gifts are culturally appropriate. The dolls she chooses are black, "something most South African girls have never seen," she says. Subsequent scenes in South Africa depict former South African president Nelson Mandela, whom Oprah describes as her mentor and a "beloved and inspiring hero." Mandela's presence symbolizes a benediction, but not a solemn one. The aged Mandela is celebrating with the children, swaying to music. After the enthusiasm of hundreds of children at parties, the tone shifts. A tent collapses at one of the gift-giving events, injuring ten people. The footage depicting the collapse is candid, but it is also edited. After the accident, Oprah leads a prayer service. "All of us feel blessed to have not only survived this experience but to come through it strengthened with a greater realization of how quickly, how short, how exacting life can be," Oprah says.

After more festive scenes of gift giving, the tone turns solemn. "We'll show you the reason why none of us can turn our backs on these children," Oprah says. The subject is AIDS and AIDS orphans in South Africa. More than once in the program Oprah tells viewers that the devastation of AIDS in Africa is something they are likely unaware of. So the program is giving them an education about the prevalence and impact of the disease on people in South Africa, especially children. "The conditions under which many children in this world live are simply unacceptable," Oprah says. "Think about the potential if we, all of us, give them the chance they deserve."

As Oprah well knows, television puts human faces on grim statistics. Oprah's visit to an orphanage introduces Marcus, a young boy diagnosed with HIV. After antiretroviral treatment, uncommon in South Africa, he tests HIV-negative. "You're our little victory boy," Oprah tells the boy as she holds him. "That is an amazing story."

Several other children's stories are told. Esona visits her mother, who has been hospitalized for an AIDS-related illness. Lying in her hospital bed, the woman appears thin yet dignified. She and Oprah talk. At the end, Esona lingers to hug her mother good-bye. Oprah then informs viewers that the mother died three months later. She was twenty-nine. "AIDS has become the defining moral issue of our times," Oprah says, quoting musician and activist Bono.

With their backpacks and school uniforms and big smiles, South Africa's AIDS orphans in desperate straits could also be the kids down the suburban block. Oprah makes it appear that way. "These children are just children," Oprah says. "They're just like yours." They are not starving or emaciated; their images do not repulse or induce guilt. They are intended to convey a sense of normalcy about South African children who are experiencing a crisis that is remote to most viewers. By making a remote cause easy to relate to and empathize with, Oprah can avoid preaching. She offers informative entertainment with a value and goal. She can change lives without earnestly announcing that she is changing lives.

As so many of her stories do, these pack an emotional punch. This is what AIDS orphans look like. Yet while the stories are sad, they are neither relentless nor paralyzingly discouraging. On the contrary, if you give you will get something back: joy. "What I wanted you to see is the extreme need for us, everybody who hears this today, to do what you can to help—and the extreme joy that helping brings when you give just a little bit of yourself," Oprah says. You can do something; in fact you should. And do it today, thank you. The address for Oprah's Angel Network pops up on the screen. People who raise money know that asking directly for it after an immediate illustration of need will get a response.

Viewers did respond. That trip to South Africa and the "Christmas Kindness" project raised $7 million. A follow-up show broadcast December 23, 2004, updates viewers on the stories of some of the children profiled the year before, and reports on how Angel Network funds were spent. It also shows the involvement of celebrities such as actor Brad Pitt and musician Alicia Keys with AIDS in South Africa. The charitable efforts of people who aren't rich and famous are also depicted; a film producer says she went to Nigeria to do AIDS prevention work, and a photographer visits a school in South Africa to shoot pictures for students. They talk about the joy of giving and getting back. Oprah also interviews Archbishop Desmond Tutu, a living symbol of overcoming adversity in South Africa. The show's message is one of gratitude and optimism for the future in spite of formidable odds.

Using Her Life

Oprah has talked consistently throughout her career about making a difference and giving back. She writes in the April 2003 issue of *O, The Oprah Magazine*, about her trip to South Africa: "I've always encouraged giving. Using your life. Teaching what you learn. Extending yourself in the form of service." She has repeatedly talked about using television to make a positive difference in people's lives, especially for those who have experienced abuse. Television can inspire or teach or "make a connection." In a show broadcast on Christmas Eve 1999, featuring inspiring "spirit stories" for the holidays, Oprah says to a guest whose decision to care for a troubled child was inspired by an episode of the show, "I love TV! I love that television can do that. I love television that can make a connection like that."

Oprah is also using her own life. Her stature rests in part on her humanitarian reputation. The list of groups she has benefited is long. She received the first-ever Bob Hope Humanitarian Award in 2002 from the National Academy of Television Arts and Sciences, which awards Emmys, and the Marian Anderson Award from the city of Philadelphia in 2003. Both honors recognized her philanthropic work.

Her emphasis on charity is visible in Oprah's Angel Network, begun in 1997, which has raised $27 million from viewers and other supporters. Profits from souvenir merchandise sold through Oprah's Boutique benefit the Network. Recipients of Angel Network funds are regularly featured on the show and at the Web site. Readers and viewers are invited to give feedback about Angel Network recipients, which gives Oprah's organization the chance to gather additional material, whether positive or negative, about groups that receive funds. From 2000 to 2003, Use Your Life awards were given by the Angel Network to individuals and organizations making a difference in people's lives and communities. (The awards, totaling $6 million, were also supported by actor-philanthropist Paul Newman, whose Newman's Own product line distributes all profits to charity, and Jeff Bezos, founder of Amazon.com.)

Oprah also funds the private Oprah Winfrey Foundation, to which she contributed $43.5 million in 2003 and which made $6.4 million in gifts that year. Since 1989, when she first gave it $1 million, she has given or pledged a total of $12 million to Morehouse College, the historically black men's college that is the alma mater of Martin Luther King Jr. In 2004, she gave $1 million to the National Underground Railroad Freedom Center, a Cincinnati museum showcasing the secret route that led black slaves to freedom. She also narrates an educational film shown there. In 2002, the foundation gave $2.5 million to New York University's Wagner School of Management to establish the Oprah Winfrey Scholars Program for African Women. In 2000, she gave $10 million to A Better Chance, a Boston-based organization that places gifted minority students in top high schools. She is also the organization's national spokesperson. In 1997, Oprah challenged her television viewers to volunteer for Habitat for Humanity, the organization that builds affordable housing through homeowner and volunteer labor. By 1999, almost two hundred houses had been built. This list is not exhaustive. Education, African and African American groups, and children's and women's organizations have been the beneficiaries of Oprah's considerable philanthropy.

Putting a Face on Need

Oprah's Web site offers opportunities to donate or volunteer. It gives information about more than two hundred charitable organizations that have had exposure over the years on the show. When the tsunami disaster of 2004 claimed more than 150,000 lives in countries bordering the Indian Ocean, the Web site listed relief organizations and contained a message board for viewers to post thoughts and prayers. More than five thousand viewers from around the world posted messages, many offering prayers. Interior designer Nate Berkus, a frequent Oprah guest, was vacationing in Sri Lanka and survived the tsunami. A number of posts observed that Berkus gave a face to the tragedy for them. The first show taped after the disaster aired January 5, 2005. It begins with information about what happened and about Berkus's condition. Oprah notes that "155,000 members of our human family are gone," and goes on to refer viewers to the Web site for a list of relief organizations. "There is a lot we can do," she says. Berkus appears in person on a January 17, 2005, show, which features him and four other survivors whom he met during the ordeal. Oprah asks what lesson the tsunami taught them. "We owe it to ourselves and to the people that lost their lives to make the most of what we have left," answers Ani Naqvi, a former producer for the British Broadcasting Corporation. At the conclusion of the show, Oprah announces a $1 million donation from her public charity, Oprah's Angel Network, to be given to three organizations assisting in the rebuilding of Sri Lanka. "Together, if we choose to be, we all can be the ultimate force of nature," Oprah says.

Other shows about giving chronicle the extraordinary efforts and decisions of ordinary people. The April 4, 2001, show, "All for One and One for All," features a woman who split $87 million in lottery winnings with twelve coworkers, and an English businessman who paid off the mortgages of seven employees who helped him rebuild after his factory burned. Also featured is a nine-year-old boy who raised $210,000 to build wells in Africa. Oprah tells him, "You are really living proof that one person, and it doesn't matter how old that person is, can make a difference in the world." Most of the people featured on this show were articulate about their motives, and their stories spoke the lesson of generosity. Oprah often states the moral of the show—"what I want you to get"—for viewers, but on this day the stories preach themselves.

The December 8, 1999, show, "The Courage to Give," opens with a line Oprah has repeatedly invoked to promote generosity: "It is the one thing I absolutely know for sure. You receive from the world what you give to the world." She calls this "the golden rule, the law of karma." The life stories on the show are intended to inspire giving and to demonstrate that giving pays back the giver. Eight separate stories are presented, and some of the givers shown have inspired others to follow their example. Jackie Waldman, the author of the book *The Courage to Give*, which Oprah says inspired the show, is shown helping three women carry out their intention to volunteer. "I've always thought about volunteering, but I just never got around to it or never knew exactly, like, where to go," said one woman. These instructions—how to find a place where volunteers are needed—are a how-to for anyone who has ever stated that good intention. The show closes with a reminder of how to get more information.

The July 25, 2002, show, "What Would You Do for a Friend?" features a man who donated a portion of his liver to a friend, and the story of Abe Zelmanowitz and Ed Beyea, both of whom died in the collapse of the World Trade Center in 2001 when Zelmanowitz stayed with Beyea, a quadriplegic wheelchair user. This show delivers inspiration and also calls for reflection and self-examination. Oprah says, "We'll make you question yourself. What would you do for a friend?"

Too Much?

Oprah is known for her holiday "favorite things" shows, broadcast almost every holiday season since 1996. On these programs, Oprah names and gives away to her audience products she enjoys. In 2004, she filled the audience for her annual giveaway with three hundred teachers. She opens the program by talking about teaching and her own aspirations to teach. "I love teachers," she says, and several clips from past programs show her saying much the same thing. "This entire hour is a tribute to teachers who give and give," she continues. The items given away on the show included a washer and dryer, a trip to an Arizona spa, and a laptop computer. The nineteen goodies were worth $15,000; each audience member received that bonanza. "It is a blessing to be able to do all this," Oprah says at the show's conclusion. "My Christmas prayer is that love will spread through every heart." Information about the 2003 "favorite things show," available at the Web site, includes a section about giving by volunteering.

The theme of her show's 2004–2005 season is "Wildest Dreams Come True," but it is also about giving. "This season on my show," writes Oprah in her "What I Know for Sure" column in the November 2004 issue of *O, The Oprah Magazine*, "I wanted to make giving a theme. What I most hope to give people is a chance to do better and be better." She then writes about giving away $7.8 million in new cars to 276 audience members on her season opener. "I wanted the force of the gift to be about not just the cars but the essence of what it means to share what you have," she continues.

"I have worlds of good to do," she told *USA Today* in an interview that appeared the day after the car giveaway show. "What I really wanted for myself and the audience was to feel the intention of giving."[1]

The big car giveaway was a lightning rod for cynics, many of whom noted that the real giver was in fact General Motors, which donated the cars and received attention when the giveaway made headlines ("Car Giveaway on Oprah Winfrey Show Is Publicity Bonanza for Star, GM"; "276 New Cars for the Fans in Oprah Ratings Drive"). Two weeks later, in a follow-up show, Oprah addressed the issue directly, describing the giveaway as "my kindness and GM's generosity." She said that winners were responsible for paying taxes on their cars and had been so informed, a fact that also had some tongues wagging. The show then features videotaped clips of winners thanking Oprah and describing how the car has made a difference in their lives. "Gratitude, I love gratitude," Oprah says.

Some saw publicity, some saw generosity, some saw shrewdness in Oprah's ability to redistribute the resources of a large corporation. "It was astounding to me how people attacked Oprah," says Kellie A. McElhaney, executive director of the Center for Responsible Business at the University of California, Berkeley. Suspicion of companies and people who want to do good runs deep in the culture, especially when those companies and people are rich and powerful. "We like to knock people off pedestals," McElhaney says.

McElhaney admires what the talk show host does with her assets. "There are a lot of things she could do with her power, wealth, and visibility other than build schools in Africa," she says. McElhaney also watches the show occasionally and experiences it as a positive force, as so many viewers do. "A majority of times I end up really feeling good about watching that show," she says.

Oprah's generosity has been criticized as self-serving and consumerist. Yet she has consistently used her public pulpit to remind people to give, to showcase life stories of people who have chosen to give, and to make giving rewarding. She has given millions to charity and established a charity, Oprah's Angel Network, to funnel her viewers' charitable impulses. In 2003, *Ebony* magazine speculated that Oprah might be the biggest philanthropist in African American history, noting that her private foundation had donated $32 million to African and African American causes.[2] In 2004, *BusinessWeek* estimated her lifetime giving at $175 million.[3] Not only does Oprah preach generosity, she practices it too.

Chapter Nine

Oprah Explores Forgiveness

*F*orgiveness has been a recurring theme in Oprah Winfrey's work. Invariably compelling, often surprising, always emotional, forgiveness holds drama. It makes a good story. Oprah regularly features victims. Some of them have chosen to forgive those who wronged them. Through forgiveness, someone who has been wronged stops being a victim. But forgiving isn't always appropriate. Oprah has done shows over the years about forgiveness or self-forgiveness, but rarely in connection with child or spouse abusers. Some wrongs go very deep.

Ethicists and religious thinkers say that forgiveness can never be compelled. Like many who have studied forgiveness, Anglican bishop Richard Holloway never says one *ought* to forgive: "We do not have the right to order people to act in ways of which they are incapable, such as commanding them to forgive."[1] Oprah is never that direct. Through the life stories presented on *The Oprah Winfrey Show*, she demonstrates how forgiveness is a choice some people have made. She invites viewers to explore it, to think about it—"think about it differently," as she often describes the goal of her work.

Her shows explore the circumstances of forgiveness: how it happens; what happens when it is, or is not, granted. They explore extraordinary forgiveness, even though not everyone will be a crime or abuse victim, and ordinary forgiveness, which applies to everyone who makes a mistake, whether it is more or less serious. A cheating spouse is a common challenge. Sometimes a person forgives another; sometimes the problem is self-forgiveness. Sometimes forgiveness has limits. These stories are reminiscent of medieval morality plays, retold as contemporary allegories in which Everyman, or Everywoman, meets Forgiveness. Over time and with repeated telling, Oprah has gotten better at making her point: This is what forgiveness looks like. She has taken a lot of looks at the subject.

As on so many of the Oprah shows dealing with people with problems and how they resolve those problems, ordinary people share their life stories illustrating forgiveness, like someone providing religious witness. The most jaw-dropping stories about forgiveness come from victims of horrific crimes who have come to terms with what happened and have forgiven the perpetrators. On the April 22, 2002, show, "Incredible Stories of Forgiveness," victims of crime speak for themselves. No experts on forgiveness appear on this show. The guests are the experts. Chip and Jody Ferlaak's four-year-old daughter was killed by a suicidal driver. Sharmeta Lovely was severely injured in a beating from an attacker who also killed her boyfriend. When she was twelve, Leslie Douglass was assaulted by two men who invaded her family's home and shot her, her brother, and their parents. Her parents died.

Oprah welcomes her viewers and previews the point of the show, its moral. She often explains to viewers why she has chosen to do a particular show, especially when it may be upsetting or somehow controversial. On this show, she says, viewers will be moved. "For many of us, the criminals who committed these horrible acts would be beyond forgiveness, but today you're going to witness some of the most incredible stories ever of what most people could never get over, and—and hopefully it will help you think of the little penny-ante things in your own life that you can't get over," she says.

Each guest relates details of her or his story, making the scene vivid and heart wrenching. These ordinary people have had experience with catastrophe and wrestled with profound questions: Why me? How do I go on? Oprah wants viewers to draw meaning for their own lives that they can use even if these horrible things don't happen to them. The questions—and their answers—can be relevant for everyone even if the circumstances differ. "The next time somebody does something to any of us—any of us who are watching or have witnessed this, we'll think about you," Oprah tells the Ferlaaks. Later in the show she addresses the audience: "Well, I don't know about you—I said this to Sharmeta Lovely during the commercial break and to Jody and Chip, 'I am the better for hearing those stories.' Don't you feel like you are the better? I don't know if I have what you have. But I am the better for hearing your stories."

The language on this show for the most part is religiously neutral. Chip and Jody Ferlaak told a magazine that they had been asked by producers to avoid specifically Christian language in relating their story so that its message of forgiveness would be apparent to people of different faiths.[2] The most explicitly religious exchange happens between Oprah and Sharmeta Lovely, when Oprah closes Lovely's story with the enthusiastic request, "Preach, girl. Preach to me. Amen!" God is implied, sometimes explicitly mentioned, in these life testimonies. But the life lesson—forgiveness in action rather than its divine teacher or exemplar—is the focus. The lack of religious specificity gives the lesson broad relevance. It might even fit those who don't believe in God.

Self-Forgiveness

Forgiveness is profound enough to offer lots of avenues to explore. Sometimes it involves others; sometimes it involves oneself. The November 15, 2000, show, "How to Forgive Yourself," includes Rabbi Irwin Kula, who fills the role of moral expert, questioning and interacting with three guests. Christy Robel's six-year-old son was killed in a 2000 carjacking. Her story does not involve forgiving the criminal. Rather, the mother cannot forgive herself for not having prevented her son's murder. She feels responsibility for having briefly left him in the car when she stopped to get him a drink, then could not free him from the car before the carjacker sped away. Kula tells Robel that understanding why something happened is not important to forgiveness. Along with the rabbi, Oprah has plenty to say. "And I think part of it is understanding your life is bigger than that moment. Your life is bigger than your son's death," she tells the mother. Later Oprah draws out the lesson for others, since few will face this exact situation: "I think this is really important for everybody who is going through this—you know, not to live in the 'What if?' because the 'What if?' is the past, and you recognize that that cannot be changed, but what next?" In this lengthy exchange, the three speakers say "Right" to one another a lot. They understand, and saying "Right" lubricates their conversation.

Oprah introduces another family, whose story has some positive resolution and who can serve as example and model. Teresa Birch, a mother, fell asleep while driving her six children, and the resulting car accident killed three of those children. Teresa also says she feels responsible. She uses religious language in describing her response to the accident. "And knowing that while we were in that dark place and hurting so badly, we felt a lot of love from God, you know, just filling us and feeling very strong and intense and knowing that—people would say, 'Oh, you'll get to be with your kids again someday,' and we have a lot of faith that that's true." She also talks about being a daughter of God, a point the rabbi amplifies in discussion.

In her wrap-up remarks to the audience, Oprah speaks not about forgiveness but justice. She tells viewers in Kansas City, Missouri, that the man whose carjacking killed Robel's son faces trial. "I think it is the responsibility of the citizens of Jackson County to make sure that true justice is served in this case. . . . When the case comes to trial, Kansas City, Jackson County, you know what to do."

Justice and forgiveness can collide. When the wrong done involves spouse or child abuse, Oprah comes down hard on the side of the victim. On the February 18, 2005, show, "Oprah Goes to Prison," Oprah interviews Aaron Estes, a North Carolina pastor convicted of murdering his wife in 2003. "You're going to have to do better than that," Oprah says to him as he recounts his version of events. On this show, Oprah's interest is not in closure or reconciliation but in the question of spousal violence.

Ethicists and people who have experienced crime wrestle with the demands of justice. Some of them say that those who are alive cannot forgive on behalf of those who have died, that it is presumptuous, that it dishonors the memory of those who have been killed. Forgiveness cannot be cheap. It cannot paper over or ignore a wrong.

"After Violence, the Possibility of Healing," an article in the April 2004 issue of *O, The Oprah Magazine*, explores restorative justice, a process that brings together offenders and victims in face-to-face meetings. Victims have a chance to ask questions; offenders are given a chance to see the harm they have done. The process is intended to help victims and to bring about awareness in offenders. With its emphasis on justice for crime victims, the point of the process is not forgiveness, but forgiveness may occur.

Unlike much else of what Oprah presents, the process of restorative justice relates to a system—the criminal justice system—and she suggests changes in it to help change an individual, whether the crime victim or even the criminal. Critics of Oprah tend to say she relies too much on individual changes of heart rather than social change, that her approach psychologizes what are really social problems. Others argue, though, that Oprah has helped to change how American society thinks about problems within families.[3] Matters that were formerly kept secret or regarded as outside the realm of criminal justice, as merely "domestic," now receive attention. Many feminists and advocates for women's issues give Oprah high marks for this same reason: that she has consistently and persistently brought concerns important to women and families into public light.

A Closer Look at "Thinking Differently"

The March 9, 1993, show, "I Killed Somebody and Can't Live with Myself," explores both self-forgiveness and apology for a mistake. The show presents four dramatic stories recounted by people who made errors in judgment that had grave consequences. One man fatally shot his fiancée by accident; a second caused an accident that severed the legs of a coworker; two others struck pedestrians with their cars, in one instance fatally and in the other case injuring a child.

Oprah presents the moral at the show's beginning. "That's what we are talking about today—how to overcome those haunting memories and guilt of hurting or killing someone by mistake," she says. This promises a happy ending: Memories can be overcome and here's how. To underscore the optimistic direction the show will take, she offers a preview to keep viewers watching. "Later we're going to have a special reunion between a woman who's never had the chance to apologize to the six-year-old little girl that she ran over," she says.

The first two stories are more detailed and provide greater drama. Oprah is a discreet interviewer who doesn't talk very much or ask many questions. She says "Mm-hmm" or "Uh-huh" forty-six times. Many of her questions are short and specific, intended to elicit or clarify a detail ("And how did you hear of her death?" "And she died?" "He was talking about his son?"). Oprah is an empathetic listener whose prompts help draw out the story.

Oprah can then introduce an expert to explain what is going on and provide a solution. The expert this day is grief therapist Jane Middelton-Moz, who explains the psychology of grief and gives advice. Talking it over is required, even if it's painful. The therapist provides a final answer at the end of the program, when Oprah is talking with the audience, fielding questions and comments. The therapist can also address questions and problems presented by the audience, and Oprah turns to her for a show-ending summary: "Bottom line is, Jane?" Middelton-Moz responds, "Talk about it."

In the final story, a woman tells her account of striking a six-year-old girl with her car and seriously injuring the child. Oprah interrupts this story with a question she regularly asks about stories involving injury: Why haven't you two talked? Guests usually answer that authorities have told them not to contact the injured party. In this story, Oprah immediately gets the two sides together, bringing the young accident victim and her mother onstage. The driver apologizes and presents a stuffed animal to the child she struck and injured, to audience applause. Like the chorus in a Greek drama, the audience watches, symbolizing society. This is good behavior intended to repair the wrong. Oprah has been fairly direct even while she has also been an apparently neutral and empathetic listener.

The Role of Apology

The ethical and practical challenge of living with the consequences of your own or someone else's error or wrong has been the subject of lots of shows over time. Some of them are packaged as practical, "how-to" information, such as "How to Forgive Yourself" and "How to Apologize." The July 25, 1996, show, "I'm Sorry Day," explores apology and the part it can play in forgiveness. The show's title sums it up. After an opening montage of video clips highlighting dramatic lines from guests on the upcoming show interspersed with short melodramatic comments from Oprah ("An abusive father regrets his past," "But should his daughter forgive?") designed to draw viewers in, Oprah's first speech announces the goal for the show. "Well, today is 'I'm sorry' day, and we're trying to give people a chance to ask those they've wronged for forgiveness," she says. "Watch the show and find, perhaps, the courage to apologize."

This show presents seven stories of different wrongdoing in which apologies are warranted: childhood abuse, crime, rudeness, personal injury. The first story, the longest, is a story of a father's childhood physical abuse of his daughter and their subsequent estrangement. Interviewing the daughter, Oprah asks her why she needs to forgive her abuser. "I don't know that I've ever felt that I needed to forgive, but I've heard it from a lot of people, and my mother's always told me growing up that I needed to let go of some of the anger . . . and to forgive in terms of making my life a better life." Oprah then brings out the father, who apologizes and asks his daughter's forgiveness. When Oprah asks for her reaction, the daughter says, "It doesn't change, you know, anything that ever happened." Before the family's story is over, the daughter's husband has been brought onstage, along with the couple's infant son. "That's a good beginning," Oprah says.

Oprah has staged an apology—literally. It looks awkward and halting but appropriate. It is a little morality play with a relatively happy ending. There are no hugs that strain believability, but the baby at the end neatly symbolizes new beginnings. This is quintessential Oprah. She presents a story that seems natural and sincere, with moral values that are reinforced, steering toward a goal of change with questions that probe emotions ("How do you feel about that?"), all within a television time frame that fits between commercial breaks.

"How to Apologize," from October 23, 1998, is related to events in the news. In walking out onstage, Oprah immediately addresses the audience: "Anybody here find it easy to say 'I'm sorry'? You do? You do?" She then asks the audience if they think President Bill Clinton's apology for his affair with political intern Monica Lewinsky, in the headlines all that year, was sincere. The audience says no.

Oprah has some powerful life stories to present and introduces "a remarkable testimony to the power of apology." Cindy Griffiths has forgiven Verma Harvey, who while driving drunk in 1996 killed Griffiths's mother and daughter, a crime for which the driver pleaded guilty and received probation. Griffiths refers explicitly to God four times as the source of her ability to forgive. "What I gave is what has been given to me, Oprah. And I have found such love, unconditional love, in God." Oprah is also explicit: "I understand the whole God connection, so I understand that's the only way you could." She also explicitly asks the driver, Harvey, about her faith and belief in God, which Harvey affirms.

The language on this show is especially religious. Oprah calls this story a "testimony," a word commonly used by religious people to talk about God's direct action in their life. In discussing this story of forgiveness with guest psychologist Marilyn Mason, Oprah three times calls it "amazing grace," either a conscious or unconscious allusion to the Christian hymn, a song of the redemption of a "wretch." Oprah says to the psychologist, "You've gotta have something bigger than yourself going on . . . to be able to do that [i.e., forgive]." Later in the show, Aaron Lazare, a psychiatrist whom Oprah introduces as an "apology expert," provides a laundry list of elements that make an effective apology: acknowledge, explain, express remorse, and make it right.

Shows about forgiveness and apology mix religiously tinged language, expert commentary, and examples from ordinary people describing their experience in plain language. The divinity that some of her guests see at work in their stories is sometimes named as God. This belief is part of the explanation of forgiveness and apology, along with the analysis offered by psychology experts. What it adds up to is a nonsectarian picture that says both that forgiveness is God-driven and that "morally it is the right thing to do," in psychologist Mason's words. Theology is present but not primary. God is acknowledged as necessary, but the language doesn't insist on that. It's soft sell. Oprah jokes in general language about being taught by human example: "Cindy [Griffiths] is my role model now. . . . I'm just going to go to that Cindy place."

"None without Sin"

The authority of religious language and experts is used on the September 14, 1998, show, "Cheating Husband: What Would You Do?" Clinton's affair with Monica Lewinsky is the subject of the show, but Oprah has material to spare for this subject, a perfect mix of public and private affairs. Guests include Effi Barry, ex-wife of former Washington mayor Marion Barry, whose troubles included conviction on drug charges as well as public revelations of womanizing. "Is adultery now the forgivable sin?" Oprah asks at the show's beginning. Effi Barry tells Oprah that her faith and spirituality helped her get through her husband's trial. In their lengthy conversation, Barry says, "And then when I couldn't cry anymore, I just said, 'Lord, it's on you. I can't—I just can't handle this.'" A less famous couple dealing with adultery, Dean and Sandy, also talk very explicitly about faith saving their marriage. "And I can truthfully say the only thing that brought the reconciliation in our marriage was Christ," Sandy says.

Marriage counselor Gary Smalley is one of the expert guests on this show. Smalley has written several popular books about marriage and family relationships, and is particularly popular with evangelical Christians, though his books appeal beyond that audience. The Rev. Donald Bell, another guest and family relationship expert, says the country's attitude toward Clinton's affair is "morally schizophrenic." Oprah even quotes a lengthy statement by Billy Graham on morality and leadership, and then steers the conversation with Bell toward forgiveness. Bell runs a program for men "apologizing to women for the, quote, sins they've committed against them." Oprah brackets the term "sins," using it gingerly, but returns to it later in asking Bell to clarify what he means. "We all have forgiven," she says, ". . . because we know that there's none of us without sin ourselves."

This show was part of Oprah's "Change Your Life TV" season (1998–1999), which began only a week earlier. The season consciously featured spiritual themes, and shows concluded with "Remembering Your Spirit" segments intended to inspire through life stories or inspirational words. Concluding this show about adultery and marriage, Oprah says on "Remembering Your Spirit" that she had originally intended to conclude with a prayer. Instead she calls for a moment of silence in which everyone can "ask for divine guidance and clarity." In thanking guest Effi Barry at the show's end, Oprah thanks her for "the light that shines through you that we know comes from a higher source than yourself." As this show demonstrates, Oprah draws on Christian roots and references even while attempting to broaden her language to speak to all viewers regardless of their religious vocabulary, or lack of it.

Follow-up: Recycling, Revising, Realism

Cindy Griffiths's tale of forgiveness of a drunken driver is repeated four years later on the April 22, 2002, show, "Incredible Stories of Forgiveness." Introducing an edited version of the story, Oprah talks about the role of faith in her guest's life. "I'm in awe of this mother's faith, another person who is living the faith and not just talking about it, and her ability to forgive," she says. Oprah has a lot of material that can be repeated or updated. Earlier tapes can be used as background and edited to hone in on the intended point. The rerun uses this dialogue:

Oprah: I understand the whole God connection, so I understand that's the only way you could [forgive]. But weren't you angry at first?

Griffiths: I wasn't angry at her. I was angry—if you could— you know, if—if evil was tangible and personified, I was angry at evil. I was angry that there was such a thing as death. I was angry that there was such a thing as—as—children growing up with such low self-esteems [*sic*] that they don't care what they do when they're older and they can do something like this.

Their conversation mixes the psychological or emotional, such as angry feelings and children with low self-esteem, and the theological—the "God connection," the personification of evil, the inevitability of human death. The words don't sound profound, but they are persuasive and realistic in their simplicity, hesitation, and emotion. Everyone has a lesson to learn, as Oprah reminds us in concluding the show: "I hope that this makes you think about whoever in your life you need to forgive or seek forgiveness from and will think differently about it as a result of seeing these people who were the heroes of their own lives."

Unfortunately for people and for TV, not all stories end heroically or happily ever after. "How to Apologize" on October 23, 1998, follows up with the man who apologized two years earlier on another show for abusing his daughter. "I'm not going to say she's jumping into my arms," he says on the later show. But, he adds, they visit. The follow-up allows Oprah to repeat earlier material and add to it, which enhances the realism of the life stories she presents. Life goes on; dieters or addicts have lapses, as Oprah herself has literally embodied. Over time and with repeated themes and guests, Oprah not only gets more material, but she also has room to grow and change, which adds variety and interest to her show.

Oprah also has other media to present the message to different audiences or to provide additional information that TV can't provide or doesn't have time for. At the Web site, visitors can explore the topic of forgiveness further and find practical things to do. Click on "rituals for forgiveness" and find instruction in different practices: "atonement, meditation/reflection, use a mantra, journaling." The language used to describe these practices is inclusive: "Wisdom traditions" and "many religions" have used these techniques. Or viewers can discuss the show on bulletin boards. The Web site offers resources and extends the experience that Oprah provides.

The world's religions talk about forgiveness as part of the wisdom they offer on how to live. No religion has a monopoly on this teaching, so the topic crosses religious lines. It is moral and psychological. Forgiveness challenges: How can someone who has been wronged forgive? Does forgiving mean excusing or forgetting a wrong? Must one forgive? Forgiveness involves a number of issues: justice, physical healing, psychological peace of mind, love, memory, responsibility, moral judgment. Where is the balance between justice and mercy? That question predates TV.

Raised in the Christian tradition, where forgiveness is a central part of the teachings of Jesus, and publicly admitting to mistakes as part of her life story, forgiveness must be a powerful value for Oprah. In *On Forgiveness*, Anglican bishop Richard Holloway says that forgiveness reclaims the future by redeeming a past that has been determined by irreversible choices. "The real beauty and power of forgiveness is that it can deliver the future to us."[4] This says in moral language what Oprah often talks about psychologically. She talks about forgiveness as giving up the wish for the past to be different.

South African archbishop Desmond Tutu, a friend of Oprah's, presents a similar argument in *No Future without Forgiveness*, in which he reflects on his experience chairing his country's Truth and Reconciliation Commission. The commission was empowered to grant amnesty to individuals who were willing to acknowledge and accept responsibility for crimes they committed during apartheid rule. It required the disclosure of secret wrongs to victims' families and to the larger society. Tutu writes that forgiveness expresses faith in the future: "We are saying here is a chance to make a new beginning. It is an act of faith that the wrongdoer can change."[5]

These small dramas of liberation from the past into a new future are Oprah's forte. To teach people to think a little differently about forgiveness, she has learned to use television very effectively. As all good storytellers know, showing is better than telling. Oprah doesn't have to get preachy when stories can testify for her. Forgiveness is one of those possibilities Oprah reminds us about.

Chapter Ten

Oprah Is a Reminder Service

*I*n the past year, whenever I told anyone I was working on a book about Oprah, their first question invariably was "So have you talked to her?" I didn't have that privilege since Harpo Productions declined my requests for an interview. Up to a point, I understood this. I was standing in a long line of people who want some time or commercial blessing from Oprah. As Oprah's friend Gayle King told *Fortune* magazine, "Everybody's thinking, 'I gotta get a piece of that Oprah brand.' "[1]

What was behind people's curiosity, though, interested me. Everyone seems to want to know: What's she *really* like? Is that stuff on TV for real? After steeping myself in her work, this is how I answer that question: I think Oprah tells the truth, mainly. I also know that her show is edited and its audience is "warmed up," that is, the studio audience's pump is primed beforehand to encourage reaction. Yet I think Oprah, and the admiration she inspires, is real enough. Since the beginning of her broadcasting career in 1971, she has struck an emotional, empathetic chord with millions of people through her genuineness and warmth. She has done so on television, a medium that features semi-scripted "reality TV" and talk shows on which a host like Oprah, with her gifts of spontaneity and directness, can seem to be addressing you personally. Yet as she has said on shows, she's not your friend. You can't call her in the evening.

I can't know if Oprah is *really* real because I don't know her. What I know for sure, to borrow her phrase, is that what she *does* is real. She acknowledges people's dignity and intelligence, reminding—sometimes prodding—them about what they already know. Oprah is a reminder service. If you really like her, she becomes your "inner Oprah."

She often says she got to be where she is by being herself. This is true, although she also knows how to act like herself. Although she began her career as a talk show host in Baltimore and Chicago, Oprah Winfrey first came to national attention in 1985 as an actress, when she appeared in the movie *The Color Purple* and was nominated for an Academy Award for best supporting actress. Her gift is to be herself, enjoy it, and to know how to act like herself. Although I knew she wasn't my friend, I found myself caring about her, staring closely at her face on TV. Is she tired today? Irritable? Is this an off day? We all have them. One day she acknowledged a cold, apparent in her voice. Anybody who has dragged herself to work while ill can relate to that—another imperfection that makes Oprah seem so human. On went the show, day after day.

"TV Oprah"—the Oprah image we see on the airwaves—is Oprah plus her producers plus her considerable resources plus a career's worth of broadcast experience. It is her gift—she sees it as a mission, as her commission—to appear to be the authentic core of the whole Oprah enterprise. Tell the truth and be yourself. It's easy to remember because there is nothing to memorize. Oprah can remain identifiable as Oprah, even while going through years of continuous transformation: makeovers, hairstyles, clothes sizes, and show themes and concerns. Even in the midst of constant change, somehow Oprah is a constant. She is spiritual, even though she dropped the theme "Remember Your Spirit," which she used during the show's most explicit spiritual-inspirational period from 1998 to 2000. She is no longer as frequently focused on weight loss, though it remains a ready subject for quips and identification with viewers. She changed the format of her talk show in the mid-1990s from the Phil Donahue style of the host roaming the audience to a more formal format of sitting down and interviewing guests before a live studio audience. She has gone through teams of experts, season after season: trainer Bob Greene, chefs Rosie Daley and Art Smith, psychologist Dr. Phil McGraw, self-help life coach Martha Beck, spiritual advisers Gary Zukav and Iyanla Vanzant. Through it all, through one transformation after another, she somehow remains recognizably, quintessentially Oprah. The proliferation of media sources of information—television channels, Web sites, blogs, magazines—makes skepticism about what we see and hear almost a reflex. In a landscape of skepticism and irony, Oprah offers respite. She invites you to trust her. She is conscious of having to honor that trust; if she doesn't, she loses her platform. Over the years, she has proved herself trustworthy.

Revising the Language

Over time, Oprah's terminology has evolved. In the 1990s, the terminology of spirituality—meditate, remember your spirit—was popular. In this decade, that is no longer the case. The culture has moved on, as it always does, reading books about Jesus instead of books about the spirit. Oprah both reflects and shapes that culture. Over the years she has looked for ways to express general social concerns that intersect with her own concerns, because that's her mission and that's also the way she'll make money. She can serve an audience and profit at the same time. She can do good and do well because of it. And so she uses language that is broad enough to be inclusive but not so broad as to be meaningless, and a wide audience will find at least something often enough to keep coming back.

The diversity of our religions makes the culture both nondenominational—names such as "community church" sound neutral—and multidenominational. Then there are those who belong to the fast-growing group of "nones"—the people who say they are spiritual but not religious, estimated at around 14 percent of the population. "In order to be able to pastor a pluralistic culture, you walk that fine line between the nondoctrinally specific and being too general or too broad," says Phyllis Tickle, author of *God-Talk in America.*

Oprah's spirituality talk comes from a mother tongue—the language of her own African American Christian heritage—that she inherited and was steeped in as a very young child. Until she was six, Oprah was raised in the South, on her grandmother's farm in

Kosciusko, Mississippi, and attended Faith United Mississippi Baptist Church and Sunday school there. At age three she was already reciting the story of Jesus' resurrection to the congregation. Her talent for performance won her adult admiration but the scorn of her peers, who enviously nicknamed her "the Preacher" and "Miss Jesus."[2]

The adult who grew from "Miss Jesus" has come to be an advocate of the values she learned. Bible stories teach moral lessons about what to do during the part of the week that isn't Sunday, when life questions call for immediate answers that are both practical and moral. African American Christianity has been a social as well as spiritual force. Despite the "New Age" label attached to the phase in her career in which Oprah explicitly focused on spiritual ideas, Oprah's teachings have a surprisingly traditional core. They are about everyday attitudes, responsible decision making, sharing one's gifts. They are above all practical, how-to, self-help, just-do-it. "Americans want what will work," says religion sociologist Wade Clark Roof, author of *Spiritual Marketplace: Baby Boomers and the Remaking of American Religion*.

Oprah's "New Age" talk about spirit was part of her ongoing, ever evolving attempt to find the right words for teachings she learned through religion. Her spiritually inclusive language is also intended to be unique—the language she alone speaks that makes her inspiring and distinctly herself. For marketing reasons as well as for her own sense of mission, she is putting her own stamp on the language, on the words she uses, on the culture, where the "Oprah effect" and "Oprahfication" and "She Oprah'ed it out of me" are terms that have been coined to describe her pervasive influence and style. "She's looking to find a vocabulary that's hers," says Roof. "She's not just working with the languages out there; she's helping to create those languages."

In a commencement speech at Wellesley College in 1997, when Oprah was on a platform different from her usual television platform, she tailored aspects of her basic live-your-best-life gospel to her audience, a message highly appropriate to an audience of college graduates revving up to live their best life. Offering counsel from her own experience, she cited what she had learned from one of her mentors, the writer Maya Angelou: "When people show you who they are, believe them, the first time."[3]

I have chosen to apply that to Oprah, and to take her words as a statement of what she is doing. She has always shown who she is and been clear about what she wants to do: to use TV to get people to think about things a little differently.

Meet Them Where They Are

Americans spend a lot of time in front of TV: more than seven hours daily, a far greater amount of time than they are likely to spend on activities tied to institution-based religious or spiritual life. Jesus, the Buddha, Muhammad, and other spiritual leaders acquired followers by going to where the people were: in the dusty streets and crowded squares where the public gathered to complain, shoot the breeze, and hope for a better deal. Today a lot of the public can be found in front of televisions. Scholar Jane Shattuc writes that for some feminists, the talk show has become "the public sphere" where ideas about a wide variety of topics, including seemingly "domestic" ones—fashion, child rearing, relationships—are discussed. "Talk shows are about average women as citizens talking about and debating issues and experience."[4]

Some who have studied the appeal of evangelical Christianity in America today say that its success stems from its ability to adapt to popular culture. It accepts popular culture and uses it even as it tries to shape it. "Untold numbers of religious conservatives are quite at home in the culture around them," writes social scientist Alan Wolfe.[5] The message of evangelicals about the necessity of certain key beliefs is pretty uncompromising: Jesus is the way, the truth, and the life. Yet some of the popular bearers of this message shape that message carefully so as to get people's attention and get them in the church door. Rick Warren, author of the astoundingly successful book *The Purpose-Driven Life*, neither looks nor talks like an ultraserious Christian pastor. He wears Hawaiian shirts and deliberately doesn't sound "churchy." Despite the folksy and casual exterior, however, he delivers a thoroughly Christian message: Get with the Jesus program, and it will change your life.

In a way comparable to Warren, Oprah Winfrey too is wearing popular cultural clothes. Her program mixes entertainers, news, books, lifestyle questions—the kinds of things that her audience is interested in and is talking about. She speaks their language, a kind of religiously or spiritually inclusive language that is non-denominational, affiliated with no particular religious faith. But she talks often enough about values that her audience can see she is value driven, even if the values and beliefs don't wear a specific denominational label. Oprah's clothes may bear labels, but her faith does not.

I don't know what her personal religious beliefs are. Paradoxically for such a high-profile public figure known for redefining what is public and what is private, they appear to be a private matter. But it is clear from her own words that she believes in God and is grateful to God for her success. This is humble, though many might find humble an unlikely characteristic of a woman whose face is the only image that ever appears on the cover of her glossy magazine. Oprah is not God's gift to the culture, which her critics think she thinks. Rather, she is trying to say she has God-given gifts that she uses to influence the culture. Some people might find that egocentric at best and delusional at worst. Others read it as being authentic and value driven. I accept her statement that she has said yes to God's plan for her life—a most ambitious plan.

What Oprah has successfully done is engage with the culture. She shapes it, as her book and product recommendations clearly testify. And she is shaped by it: She reflects it with her shows that seize on the topic of the day. If reality television or Bill Clinton's philandering or the murder of tourists in Miami is in the news, she will do a show on it. As a journalist, she was trained to follow the news. But she also follows her audience, her supporters. There is give-and-take. She listens to them. She clearly uses their ideas and experiences. The show depends in part on input from those who watch her. She responds to criticism, sometimes quite directly, as she did in the trash television era of the early 1990s and as she did in response to the criticism of the 2004 car giveaway. Oprah often follows up to show viewers the next chapter in a guest's story. Television may offer an opportunity to manipulate, but it also offers no hiding place for someone who is as exposed as Oprah. Guests who make confessions on national television recognize this. In interviewing several pathological liars on a March 1, 2005, show, Oprah asked one why she wanted to appear, and the guest said she needed to make it real. "There is no going back once you're on TV," Oprah tells her. "It's a way of outing yourself." The exposure of television can provide accountability. You have to do what you said you'd do.

Oprah is a comfortably charismatic figure, and most effective leaders have the gift of charisma. Her charisma becomes apparent when comparing her media platforms. The magazine may have Oprah front to back—her image on the cover and her "What I Know for Sure" column at the very end—but it doesn't have Oprah in the way the TV show has her. The magazine is infused with her tastes, concerns, and sensibility, but it lacks the ability to convey the unpretentiousness and energy that her presence on the television show conveys. Oprah's best medium is TV. She is a made-for-TV figure who has a gift to "make the connection"—one of her phrases—visually, emotionally, and with short messages made of simple words. TV multiplies her presence, expands her audience, and builds her platforms around the world.

Value Talk

There is confusion in how Americans talk today about values, especially in the wake of the 2004 presidential election that exit pollsters said hinged on "moral values." None of these pollsters, however, said what moral values were. Were they actual policy choices such as restricting abortion or restricting who can get married? Or were they a little more nebulous?

The kinds of values that Oprah teaches or presents are not so much either "spiritual" or "religious." They are American and they are related to the "American dream" and its relationship to what scholars call American "civil religion." Civil religion is often what people mean when they talk about how religion has appeared in our history and been invoked by our leaders in history. Civil religion has beliefs in God and in the action of God's will in our history. Its God-given values include liberty. It looks like the religions that people practice when they go to houses of worship or celebrate rituals or holidays.

Until around the middle 1960s, when changes in immigration laws brought appreciable numbers of people from Asia and the Middle East to America, our civil religion looked a lot like Christianity. God has a visible place in our rhetoric and history but not a dominant place in our laws, because this is not a theocracy. Colonists came to America fleeing England's state religion. America never had one.

Oprah talks about values without saying things like "Jesus is my favorite political philosopher." Oprah talks about spirituality without referring to the institutions that are set up to cultivate and nurture spirituality and without replacing those institutions. She is not really in the business of pastoring, but she can be described as pastoral. A good deal of what she is about is edifying, uplifting, and wholesome. She complements rather than rivals those institutions that promote spirituality. If she were more specific, she would be narrowcasting to smaller groups rather than broadcasting to millions in this country and around the world.

Sociologist Wayne Thompson has studied the reasons why people tune in to television preachers. He found that their TV-based religious activity complements rather than replaces the rest of their religious practices. "It's not TV instead of, it's TV in addition to, and possibly in competition with," he says. TV is one of many sources for religious or spiritual messages. Oprah is a broad influence compatible with a variety of belief systems and cultures. So she has red fans and blue fans, fans who are traditionally religious or unconventionally spiritual, fans in the Virgin Islands and in Virginia. In response to a question about politics, she told *Broadcasting and Cable* magazine:

> In this audience, there are some reds, and there are some blues, but when they come here, they become purple. The

color purple. They are looking to create a life of value for themselves. And the way to bring people together is to show them how you can do that and how your sense of values doesn't have to conflict with mine, that we can come together in such a way that you and I can both find purpose and meaning in our lives and work together.[6]

Of course, not everyone is edified. I know that when the words "Oprah" and "gospel" are included in the same sentence, some people will roll their eyes. For all the millions who trust her, others don't trust her because of her millions, because of her power and control. Those who think she can't have any kind of moral value unless she takes some very specific political position—left or right—won't find her valuable. For others, the objection is more religious than political. Oprah has worn the New Age label because of her psychological approach to problem solving that emphasizes self-esteem. She has been roundly criticized for making the spiritual too psychological, too therapeutic, too soft, too easy, too self-centered. The gospel according to Oprah doesn't appear to require some kind of doctrinal commitment or a community to ensure that the life-changing "Aha!" moment of decision is more than a new year's resolution that is quickly made in isolation and broken two weeks later.

Entertainment is not theology. Although she has been shaped by religion and provides entertainment infused with values, Oprah is not a theologian. That's somebody else's job. If faith has difficult aspects to it, talking about that is the job of religion. Oprah's gospel entertains; it's a gospel of good news. "She's been good news for this culture for a long time," says Phyllis Tickle. "If entertainment required sacrifice and discipline, it wouldn't entertain."

Oprah's gospel is a gospel of story. The Christian Gospels are also just that. Matthew, Mark, Luke, and John tell the story of the life of Jesus. Each tells it differently. But Christians understand these as Gospels according to their tellers. The Gospel according to Mark is very different from the Gospel according to John. The Gospel according to Oprah—live your best life by being grateful, generous, and honest with yourself and others—is also distinctive. But like the Christian Gospel writers, Oprah, too, has stories to tell.

No one can throw stones at her about generosity. They can't throw stones at her about her concern for victims of abuse. In ways that people can see, she walks the talk. Oprah's very visibility requires that she appear honest. She has built her image on being herself, on being open, on being reliable. To depart from those qualities would make her not Oprah. She has to continue to be trustworthy in order to continue being Oprah.

She is straightforward about her use of brand-name products. Credits for promotional consideration are listed at the end of each show, and on the air Oprah thanks those who have donated goods and services. Her use of other people's products, clearly credited, to achieve her ends is a shrewd use of resources. Television is a commercial medium, and Oprah does not pretend it is not, which is itself self-aware and honest. She has come to terms with what she needs to do to attain and maintain her platform, and she works on making those terms of the commercial broadcasting world her own terms in a language she too can live with and by.

Success by Excess

The aspect of Oprah that I find hardest to appreciate is the almost compulsive excess of it all. The stream of things to buy—decorative pillows, exercise equipment, moisturizing creams, new clothes and lots of accessories for them—doesn't bother me. Viewers can tune out what they consider irrelevant. The gospel of looking good makes sense. We live in a material world in which pretty, well-made things and bright colors can delight our senses, give us pleasure, and remind us of the earthly garden God created. Nor do I find the idea of self-care that Oprah promotes narcissistic. It makes sense to take care of your God-given body; it is the only one you'll be issued, it does wear out, it's your responsibility to take care of yourself and not abuse the resources of our health care system, and it's an awesome and mysterious God who engineered this elaborate human system that requires regular maintenance. Nor is Oprah distributing her abundant resources randomly. She makes right use of them. Those who receive material goods from Oprah are often deserving, as their stories make clear. Rock star Gwen Stefani's biggest fan gets a trip to Los Angeles for the Grammy Awards because she is a diabetic and teaches art to mentally retarded children. Illness, divorce, loss of a family member, or other tough circumstances are common in the lives of those who get picked for queen-for-a-day-style makeovers. Virtue can be rewarded, especially if Oprah hears about it. This is a good thing for her to demonstrate, and she demonstrates it often. Mother Teresa said that she didn't feed the hungry but she fed people, one by one by one. Oprah also parcels out her material bounty in this way, one recipient after another. Come back to her it does, in the form of compelling shows that interest viewers and reinforce her image as a force for goodness.

Still, I do find parts of her message mixed and confusing at times: Love yourself—but lose ten pounds. Give to receive—and don't forget to buy yourself something. Old is OK but not too old, that is, dowdy or frumpy. If you do, here's how to look ten years younger fast. Listening to and reading Oprah for a year was like always shopping, always looking for just the next better lipstick or pair of shoes, always correcting, always self-improving. A chronic edge of dissatisfaction compels the quest for satisfaction. It's a forever unquenchable desire. It's success by excess.

A guest on the February 21, 2005, show, "Look Ten Years Younger Now," illustrates the treadmill of dissatisfaction and change, of excess. Like most of the eight guests who shared their secrets of looking young, this woman said she exercised and had a decent diet. She also boasted that she ate cookie dough and whipped cream as a treat. In the context of a show intended to offer try-this-at-home strategies that have helped women stay healthy, think positively, and appear youthful, eating cookie dough seemed excessive and out of place.

The emphasis on celebrity is perhaps Oprah's most mixed message. She is obviously interested in social responsibility and is using her own, and others', visibility to raise awareness about certain issues and causes. She highlights the activities of celebrities who get involved with charity or civic improvement: athlete Lance Armstrong raises funds for cancer, singer Ricky Martin raises funds

for children, singer Alicia Keys is involved with AIDS awareness.
It is admirable that Oprah is working on restoring the function of
celebrities as role models involved in doing something more than
entertaining people. Celebrities clearly have influence on their followers' tastes in clothes, music, and movies, which Oprah is trying
to leverage into other concerns. Oprah is herself the best example.

Still, the glitter factor adds up. Matt Damon, Meryl Streep,
Johnny Depp, Barry Manilow, Jim Carrey, and Julia Roberts
(twice) in one month's stretch weigh the scale heavily in favor of
celebrity concerns, even if celebrities are interviewed because
Oprah wants to present them as just like you and me—concerned
parents who also happen to be rich and famous. Oprah tries to balance the stories of ordinary people meeting adversity in extraordinary ways with stories of celebrities who reveal the ordinary
aspects of their lives. They too get depressed and seriously ill. But
the balance has shifted. The number of Oprah's shows featuring
celebrities went up in 2004, more than doubling over 2003. This
shift came at the expense of what I classify as "personal" topics:
shows about relationships, families, makeovers.

From Values to Virtues

I think Oprah does good things, mainly. She is a force for social
good. Between philanthropy, women's empowerment, the
advancement of African American cultural contributions, the promotion of reading, and concern for children, her agenda is ambitious and commendable. She's got the power and she uses it. She
is religion dressed in fashionable street clothes, walking the walk,
meeting people where they are on weekdays, not Sundays, and
talking to them in their language, which is also hers: the language
of experience. She is about practical values and how those values
are expressed in concerns she can act on and urge others to act on:
concern for those without power, such as children; concern for
African AIDS victims without access to life-sustaining retroviral
medicines; concern for those without access to advancement
through education.

Over time, those values start to look like virtues. In commenting after the 2004 presidential election on cultural talk about values, the editors of the *Christian Century* wrote, "What matters most are not values but virtues. Values may be cited in an answer to a pollster; virtues are displayed through lives of conviction sustained over time."[7] Oprah has sustained over time her effort to uplift. This is virtuous.

The fashions of culture may change, and with them change Oprah's hair and clothing. But Oprah's underlying concern with dignity remains constant. "A lot of people think when I talk about spirituality that I'm talking some pie-in-the-sky stuff," Oprah told *Mediaweek*. "But it's not. I'm talking about how you get women to look at their lives differently and see that through the stories of other people."[8]

More recently, she expressed her goal this way in an interview with *Broadcasting and Cable* magazine: "What I now feel is reenergized by a vision of empowerment in the ability to use television in a way that I know can be even more profound. To use the connection that I have established over the years with the viewers in such a way that lets them think about themselves differently, be moved to their own personal greatness."[9]

In the way she has listened to people and helped them see themselves over the years, Oprah believes in her own viewers and their values as well as in herself. Politically, this means she believes in human dignity and equality within democracy; psychologically, she models self-esteem; morally, she argues for community improvement that flows from personal decisions you can live comfortably with, including a decision to share and give back as you have been given to. Oprah reaches her viewers through stories, which teach values. Oprah tells stories well, using a language that makes the connection. She teaches without preaching. All she has to do is talk.

Oprah has a gift for communicating things simply and convincingly. Her words are short, emotional, memorable. As do other successful public communicators, from leaders to advertisers, she stays "on message," as the phrase goes. She stays herself. She says the same thing over and over, in different ways over time to different audiences. The core messages of her gospel are clear and constant. This book has identified some of those messages: Be thankful. Give and you shall receive. Think about things a little differently. Listen to your inner voice. Know yourself. You can change. People already know these things, but in a flawed and busy world sometimes they make mistakes or just plain forget. Oprah is a reminder service.

Conclusion

The Fun Pulpit

*O*ver a family holiday dinner of Polish sausage and champagne, the subject of Oprah Winfrey came up.

My sister's niece Micki, an occupational therapist who lives in Chicago, said she had attended a taping of Oprah's show that featured makeovers of four ordinary women who were sent to the Academy Awards show.

"That was the show with the chicken lady," I said. The "chicken lady" was a Georgia chicken farmer whose work clothes included a hideous hair-engulfing cap. In her Hollywood-fueled makeover, she had gone from chickens to chic. "How'd you get those tickets, anyway? I've been trying for months."

"It was easy," Micki said. "I just sent in for those last-minute tickets that you can get by e-mail."

"Well, darn," I said. "Take me next time. So why do you like Oprah, anyway?"

"Oprah does a lot of people a lot of good," Micki said.

"I think so too," chimed in my sister Martha from across the table. Martha, who is fifty-three and works in a grocery store, is a longtime fan. "She is so generous."

All the women at the table agreed that Oprah was a force for good who used her visibility and her money to make society better. "Now if you want another opinion," said Micki, a twenty-five-year-old newlywed, "ask my husband. He just hates her."

At her beckoning, Jonathan, who had already finished dinner, slid his tall frame into a chair, rejoining us women. "Oh, Oprah," he said dismissively. "All that stuff she gives away, people give it to her. It isn't even hers, but she gets to look so generous. She just does that to get ratings and make money."

"No way," said Martha. "So what if she's rich? She helps people in Africa and all over. Besides, she works hard and she deserves it."

"She puts other people's sob stories on TV and makes a buck off them," retorted Jonathan.

"No, she was never really like that," said Jonathan's mother, Jane, who is fifty and sells cosmetics. "She was always so much better than Jerry Springer. That guy had really weird things, like transvestite couples, on his show. But Oprah did the book club, and she started a charity."

"Oprah's Angel Network," I added helpfully.

"Whatever," said Jonathan. "It's all to get you to watch."

"It is not," insisted Martha. "We know a lot about her life. She seems so real."

In the months I worked on this book about Oprah Winfrey, I took part in many conversations like this one (a real conversation with identifying details altered somewhat). Women particularly like Oprah and see her as someone whom they can respect. Since 2002, she's been more admired than Laura Bush, outranking the First Lady in Gallup's poll of most admired women.

I wrote this book because I was interested in why Oprah spoke to so many different women about so many things for such a long time. I wanted to know why so many people spoke about her in the same way: that she was authentic, real, generous. I wanted to know why she seemed to give people what religious teachings are supposed to give people: a sense of values. Mostly, though, I wanted a share of her powerful optimism. I wanted a daily booster shot to strengthen my emotional immune system against a cultural epidemic of irony.

I found myself with a year's subscription to "Pop Culture Digest." Amber Frey, Jessica Simpson, *Desperate Housewives*, Jamie Foxx—even Barack Obama, the Illinois politician who captured the public's attention like a rock star in his successful 2004 run for the Senate—joined Oprah in her studio. On many days, I found myself turning off the TV feeling energized by Oprah's enthusiasm. Yes! I could write this book!

And I did.

Just as Oprah offers a little extra conversation on her *After the Show* program on the Oxygen cable network, I would like to add at the end of this book the lessons I learned from watching her show.

Writing this book surprised me regularly. It surprised me first of all that I even did it. I was approached in 2002 about turning into a book an article I wrote about Oprah Winfrey as America's pastor. I backed away from an initial offer because I didn't want to spend a whole year of my life in front of the television with Oprah Winfrey. Three months in 2002 seemed like enough for a lifetime. But the door I thought I had closed always remained ajar. Meanwhile I kept writing about topics that people were talking about: books, Islam, pop culture. Oprah talks about what people are talking about. That's her job and her genius. I began to get more curious about what she was doing, especially since she is really into books. The prospect grew on me.

Part of the reason I was reluctant to watch Oprah is that I didn't initially get her appeal. I believed she was treating subjects in either sensational or sentimental ways to appeal to women at home watching her on TV. I was a professional who didn't have time to watch because I was writing about things that *really* mattered, not TV escapist entertainment. When I finally made the commitment to write about her work and to tune in to popular culture, I was surprised to realize what she was really doing with her TV show.

The 2004–2005 season's theme was "Wildest Dreams." She said on several occasions that it was about giving. At its best, giving looked like it was really, really fun. It was entertaining. Giving is one of the values the show stands for. Her show is about values, about ways we can care for and respect ourselves and one another and make a positive difference with our lives. She is about the very basic values I have been writing about, like gratitude and forgiveness and generosity. But they're not presented in pious, excessively earnest, preachy ways. Oprah's been about values since she started, saying that she wants to get people to think about things a little differently. I didn't just see this by myself; her fans told me this is why they like her. And it's entertaining. It's not entertainment *or* values. It's entertainment *with* values. That's not religion.

But it's compatible with religion. My friend Phyllis Tickle, who has observed the American cultural and religious scenes for a while, says Oprah is entertaining in the atrium outside the houses of worship where real religion, with doctrine, practices, and community, lives, breathes, and prays. A viewer may—or may not—go from that entryway into the house of worship.

I was surprised to realize how good an interviewer Oprah is. When she interviews celebrities, she asks personal questions that go beyond their work. When she interviews ordinary people, she takes a similar approach. Her questions can be probing. Over twenty years of her television show, she has talked to thousands of very different people. She listens. Her audience knows that. "People sense the realness," one writer wrote in 1986 at the beginning of her national career.

I was surprised that the television show could make me cry. Instead of feeling manipulated into that response, I began to wonder if my own cynicism and skepticism went a lot deeper than I realized. My tears were real. Oprah taps a soft spot in her viewers. She cries too—famously—but she is aware of the fact it can appear contrived, and she is also willing to make fun of it: If you "cry up," she says, lifting your head back far enough, your makeup won't run in ugly streaks.

I was surprised at how much I felt *a part of* the show's culture rather than *apart from* it. I was also surprised at the wide variety of subjects the show tackled, from housecleaning to South Africa. There was something for everyone, and the fans I spoke to said they appreciated that variety.

I was surprised at how many people I spoke to don't watch the show. My usual approach in writing a story is to talk to ordinary people and experts on a subject. That way I draw a picture of what something is like as people experience it and talk about it. I also include views from experts who say what this all means. The experts whose interpretations I sought about Oprah's role in the culture often began by saying they didn't watch her. This is not entirely surprising. Persons in the daytime television audience may have no job outside the home, one with a variable schedule (such as nurses), or one with hours that end before her program's time slot, or they record the show on a VCR. But the larger point is that Oprah's TV audience isn't detached, as experts are supposed to be. They feel somehow personally connected. In the case of Oprah, the real experts are the people who watch her. However personal and limited each individual viewer's opinion and experience of Oprah, these viewers nonetheless use the same words: She's real, authentic, honest, empowering.

Since I am a word person, I was probably most surprised that I began preferring the television show to her magazine. Oprah's considerable charisma comes through on television. She is engaging and touching. Her mastery of the medium of TV gave me new respect for it and its ability to reach and affect many people. It made me like television again, for what it can do: inform and entertain. Fun, fun, as Oprah might say. Not many people use the word *fun* when they're talking about religion and values. But Oprah teaches that social responsibility can be fun. She tweaked my own earnestness about what is important.

People who are familiar with the history of television or who are just plain middle-aged might remember the famous phrase that described TV as "a vast wasteland." Those words were said in 1961 by Newton Minow, who was chairman of the Federal Communications Commission. In researching this book, I read the rest of his speech. Before taking a stick to TV executives about the quality of what they were producing, Minow first praised the medium. He cited programs that were "entertaining," "moving," and "marvelously informative" and then said, "When television is good, nothing—not the theater, not the magazines or newspapers—nothing is better."[1]

TV is a vast pulpit from which Oprah offers encouragement, inspiration, and entertainment. I appreciate that she has used television to get America to pick up books and enjoy reading. I take her seriously. She does good television. She takes her pulpit seriously without being excessively serious about it.

I became convinced that Oprah's function is to be a reminder service of values, of what people already know but sometimes forget. Sometimes people call this inspiration, but I believe it goes deeper than that. Oprah reminded me to have fun, to balance with other important things in life. She reminded me why I got into writing: Like her, I like stories, and what I know for sure, to borrow the title of her magazine column, is that people like having their stories heard. It's a mark of respect. Finally, she taught me something that really surprised me: Don't wear tapered pants. They make you look fat.

How I Did This

A Note on Method

*M*y primary sources for this book were *The Oprah Winfrey Show* itself, and *O, The Oprah Magazine*. I watched the show for a year just before and during its 2004–2005 season. I also watched it for three months in 2002, when I wrote the article that this book grew from. I also read sixty transcripts of older shows. I have read around one-third of the magazine issues since publication began in 2000. Though they haven't figured in my analysis, I have also read ten of the fifty-four book club picks. I regularly observed or contributed to discussions of shows or topics at http://www.oprah .com, Oprah's Web site. I spoke to fans from different parts of the country, with different ethnicities, and from different backgrounds.

Although I called throughout an entire season of filming (and also during 2002), I never got tickets to the show. Harpo Productions declined to provide access to Oprah or to archives of older shows. It's also the case that people who work for Oprah are asked to sign lifetime confidentiality agreements regarding their work. So I had no direct access and had to work from a lot of secondary sources. A number of people I spoke to who have written about Oprah's work or impact expressed surprise that there are few serious or book-length treatments of her work. There are, however, thousands of articles in newspapers and magazines. When I used a database to retrieve them, my initial search called up more than 23,000 articles. I narrowed it from there.

The books and articles I quoted from or that influenced my thinking are cited in the bibliography. Where I used secondary sources in this book, they are noted. Otherwise I have drawn on my own interpretation, interviews, notes from shows, transcripts, or the magazine. I have cited magazine and show dates in the text to minimize the number of notes.

Acknowledgments

As I wrote earlier in this book, I learned about gratitude from Oprah. I also was reminded of the virtue of keeping things short and sweet. My wildest dream came true during Oprah's "Wildest Dreams" season: In writing this book I got more help than I dreamed possible. For their editing, time, and/or encouragement I am very grateful to: Phyllis Tickle, Jana Riess, Juli Cragg Hilliard, Marilyn Lewis, Kimberly Winston, David Gibson, Mark Pinsky, Kathryn Lofton, Jamie Phelps, Wayne Thompson, Kellie McElhaney, Ken Kuykendall, P. J. Bednarski, Jane Garrity, Juan Thomas, Sandy Hockenbury, Michael Rayford, Annah Dumas-Mitchell, Kelly Hughes, and Carol Russell. Those who attended a program I gave to the Metropolitan Chicago General Meeting of the Religious Society of Friends gave helpful feedback. Special thanks to Diane Connolly for understanding why I needed to do this.

Like gratitude, patience is a virtue. My editor at Westminster John Knox Press, David Dobson, waited years for this. My family—Bill, Margaret, and Andrew Nelson—knows that I can't keep it that short. I thank them for their editing, research assistance, listening, love, and patience. I thank God for all.

Notes

Introduction: Oprah on a Mission

1. Eva Illouz, *Oprah Winfrey and the Glamour of Misery: An Essay on Popular Culture* (New York: Columbia University Press, 2003), 5.

2. For a full discussion of sources and how they are cited in this book, see "How I Did This" on pages 98–99.

3. Margaret Bernstein, "Oprah Winfrey Tells Baptists to 'Surrender All,'" *Religion News Service*, April 18, 2005.

Chapter 1: Oprah Is Very Human

1. Illouz, *Oprah Winfrey and the Glamour of Misery*, 32–33 (emphasis in original).

2. Quoted in Shawna Malcom, "Oprah Winfrey: The Best Friend Popular Culture Ever Had," *Entertainment Weekly*, November 11, 1999.

3. Quoted in George Mair, *Oprah Winfrey: The Real Story* (Secaucus, NJ: Citadel Stars, 1998), 100.

4. A chapter in Helen S. Garson, *Oprah Winfrey: A Biography* (Westport, CT: Greenwood Press, 2004), charts the ups and downs of her weight journey.

5. Mair, *Oprah Winfrey*, 44.

6. Deborah Tannen, "Oprah Winfrey," *Time*, June 8, 1998.

Chapter 2: Oprah Acknowledges Suffering and Wants to Relieve It

1. Illouz, *Oprah Winfrey and the Glamour of Misery*, 23.

2. Ibid., 202.

3. Cecilia Konchar Farr, *Reading Oprah: How Oprah's Book Club Changed the Way America Reads* (Albany, NY: SUNY Press, 2005), 141n.

4. Mark T. Haynes, "Predicting the Effectiveness of Mediated Therapeutic Communication: Oprah's *Change Your Life TV* as a Prototype" (master's thesis, Illinois State University, 1999), 67.

5. See Jane M. Shattuc, "The Oprahfication of America: Talk Shows and the Public Sphere," in *Television, History, and American Culture: Feminist Critical*

Essays, ed. Mary Beth Haralovich and Lauren Rabinovitz (Durham, NC: Duke University Press, 1999).

Chapter 3: Oprah Provides Community

1. Farr, *Reading Oprah*, 31.
2. Ibid., 60.
3. Ibid., 54.
4. Ibid., 141n.; Richard Lacayo, "Oprah Turns the Page," *Time,* April 15, 2002.
5. See Shattuc, "Oprahfication of America."

Chapter 5: Oprah Teaches Gratitude

1. Quoted in Ann Oldenburg, "$7M Car Giveaway Stuns TV Audience," *USA Today*, September 14, 2004.
2. Robert A. Emmons and Michael McCullough, "Counting Blessings versus Burdens: An Experimental Investigation of Gratitude and Well-Being in Daily Life," *Journal of Personality and Social Psychology* 84, no. 2 (2003).

Chapter 6: Oprah Makes Things Simple

1. Lisa Granatstein, "Soul Sisters," *Mediaweek*, March 1, 2004.
2. Quoted in Sarah A. Webster, "GM, *Oprah* Team Up to Give Away Cars," *Detroit Free Press*, September 14, 2004.
3. Kathryn Lofton, "Practicing Oprah, or, The Prescriptive Compulsion of a Spiritual Capitalism," *Journal of Popular Culture* 38, no. 6 (November 2005).
4. Tannen, "Oprah Winfrey."
5. Bernstein, "Oprah Winfrey Tells Baptists to 'Surrender All.' "

Chapter 7: Oprah Listens

1. Alan Wolfe, *The Transformation of American Religion: How We Actually Live Our Faith* (New York: Free Press, 2003), 156.
2. See, e.g., Dolf Zillmann, "The Oprahization of America: Sympathetic Crime Talk and Leniency," *Journal of Broadcasting and Electronic Media*, January 1, 1999.
3. Illouz, *Oprah Winfrey and the Glamour of Misery*, 221.

Chapter 8: Oprah Teaches Generosity

1. Quoted in Oldenburg, "$7M Car Giveaway Stuns TV Audience."
2. Kimberly Davis, "Blacks Giving Back: Increasing Number Donate Large Sums to Institutions and Causes," *Ebony*, December 1, 2003.
3. "The 50 Most Generous Philanthropists," *BusinessWeek,* November 29, 2004.

Chapter 9: Oprah Explores Forgiveness

1. Richard Holloway, *On Forgiveness: How Can We Forgive the Unforgiveable?* (Edinburgh: Canongate, 2002), 76.

2. Patty Thomson, "Losing Teagan: A Story of Tragedy, Forgiveness, and Hope," *Bethel Focus*, Spring 2003, accessed at http://www.bethel.edu/alumni/Focus/Spring/03/teagan.html.

3. Illouz, *Oprah Winfrey and the Glamour of Misery*, 227–30.

4. Holloway, *On Forgiveness*, 13.

5. Desmond Tutu, *No Future without Forgiveness* (New York: Doubleday Image, 2000), 273.

Chapter 10: Oprah Is a Reminder Service

1. Quoted in Patricia Sellers, "The Business of Being Oprah," *Fortune*, March 17, 2002.

2. Mair, *Oprah Winfrey*, 8.

3. "Oprah Winfrey's Commencement Address, May 30, 1997," Wellesley College, http://www.wellesley.edu/PublicAffairs/Commencement/1997/winfrey.html.

4. Shattuc, "Oprahfication of America," 171.

5. Wolfe, *Transformation of American Religion*, 250.

6. Quoted in P. J. Bednarski, "All About Oprah Inc.," *Broadcasting and Cable*, January 24, 2005.

7. "Values and Virtues," *Christian Century*, November 30, 2004.

8. Quoted in Lisa Granatstein, "Spiritual Awakening," *Mediaweek*, April 3, 2000.

9. Quoted in Bednarski, "All About Oprah Inc."

Conclusion: The Fun Pulpit

1. Newton N. Minow, "Television and the Public Interest" (speech before the National Association of Broadcasters, Washington, DC, May 9, 1961).

Bibliography

Abt, Vickie, and Leonard Mustazza. *Coming after Oprah: Cultural Fallout in the Age of the TV Talk Show.* Bowling Green, OH: Bowling Green State University Popular Press, 1997.

Bednarski, P. J. "All About Oprah Inc." *Broadcasting and Cable,* January 24, 2005.

Bernstein, Margaret. "Oprah Winfrey Tells Baptists to 'Surrender All.' " Religion News Service, April 18, 2005.

Buckendorff, Jennifer. "The Oprah Way." *Salon,* January 24, 2005.

Collins, Patricia Hill. *Black Feminist Thought: Knowledge, Consciousness, and the Process of Empowerment.* New York: Routledge, 2000.

Copeland, Libby. "Our Lady of Perpetual Help: In the Church of Feel-Good Pop Psychology, Spiritual Rebirth Means Starting at O." *Washington Post,* June 26, 2000.

Davis, Kimberly. "Blacks Giving Back: Increasing Number Donate Large Sums to Institutions and Causes." *Ebony,* December 1, 2003.

Dickerson, Debra. "A Woman's Woman." *U.S. News and World Report,* September 29, 1997.

Emmons, Robert A., and Michael McCullough. "Counting Blessings Versus Burdens: An Experimental Investigation of Gratitude and Well-Being in Daily Life." *Journal of Personality and Social Psychology* 84, no. 2 (2003).

Farr, Cecilia Konchar. *Reading Oprah: How Oprah's Book Club Changed the Way America Reads.* Albany, NY: SUNY Press, 2005.

Garson, Helen. *Oprah Winfrey: A Biography.* Westport, CT: Greenwood Press, 2004.

Granatstein, Lisa. "Soul Sisters." *Mediaweek,* March 1, 2004.

———. "Spiritual Awakening." *Mediaweek,* April 3, 2000.

Haynes, Mark T. "Predicting the Effects of Mediated Therapeutic Communication: Oprah's *Change Your Life TV* as a Prototype." Master's thesis, Illinois State University, 1999.

Holloway, Richard. *On Forgiveness: How Can We Forgive the Unforgiveable?* Edinburgh: Canongate, 2002.

Illouz, Eva. *Oprah Winfrey and the Glamour of Misery: An Essay on Popular Culture.* New York: Columbia University Press, 2003.

Lacayo, Richard. "Oprah Turns the Page." *Time*, April 15, 2002.

Lofton, Kathryn. "Practicing Oprah, or, The Prescriptive Compulsion of a Spiritual Capitalism." *Journal of Popular Culture* 38, no. 6 (November 2005).

———. "Reading Religiously: The Ritual Practices of Oprah's Book Club." In *Oprah's Book Club: Interpretations*, edited by Cecilia Konchar Farr and Jaime Harker. Albany, NY: SUNY Press, forthcoming.

Mair, George. *Oprah Winfrey: The Real Story.* Secaucus, NJ: Citadel Stars, 1998.

Malcom, Shawna. "Oprah Winfrey: The Best Friend Popular Culture Ever Had." *Entertainment Weekly*, November 11, 1999.

McClymond, Kathryn T. "The Gospel according to Oprah." In *Religion as Entertainment*, edited by C. K. Robertson. New York: Peter Lang, 2002.

Oldenburg, Ann. "$7M Car Giveaway Stuns TV Audience." *USA Today*, September 14, 2004.

"Oprah on Oprah." *Newsweek*, January 8, 2001.

Sellers, Patricia. "The Business of Being Oprah." *Fortune,* March 17, 2002.

Shattuc, Jane M. "The Oprahfication of America: Talk Shows and the Public Sphere." In *Television, History, and American Culture: Feminist Critical Essays*, edited by Mary Beth Haralovich and Lauren Rabinovitz. Durham, NC: Duke University Press, 1999.

Tannen, Deborah. "Oprah Winfrey." *Time*, June 8, 1998.

Taylor, LaTonya. "The Church of O." *Christianity Today*, April 1, 2002.

Thomson, Patty. "Losing Teagan: A Story of Tragedy, Forgiveness, and Hope." *Bethel Focus,* Spring 2003, http://www.bethel.edu/alumni/Focus/Spring/03/teagan.html.

Tutu, Desmond. *No Future without Forgiveness.* New York: Doubleday Image, 2000.

Webster, Sarah A. "GM, *Oprah* Team Up to Give Away Cars." *Detroit Free Press*, September 14, 2004.

Welborn, Amy. "The Feel-Good Spirituality of Oprah." *Our Sunday Visitor*, January 13, 2002.

Wolfe, Alan. *The Transformation of American Religion: How We Actually Live Our Faith.* New York: Free Press, 2003.

Wuthnow, Robert. *After Heaven: Spirituality in America since the 1950s.* Berkeley: University of California Press, 1998.

Zillmann, Dolf. "The Oprahization of America: Sympathetic Crime Talk and Leniency." *Journal of Broadcasting and Electronic Media*, January 1, 1999.